LUÍS LOURENÇO

JOSÉ MOURINHO SPECIAL LEADERSHIP

PRIME BOOKS

JOSÉ MOURINHO
Special Leadership
by Luís Lourenço

This edition first published in the UK in 2014 by
Prime Books, Lda.
Rua Brito Camacho, Lt 43 – 1º Esq.
S. João do Estoril
2765-457 Estoril
Portugal
www.primebooks.pt

Originaly published in Portugal in 2010 by Prime Books

Editor: Jaime Abreu
Translation: Helena do Vale Angelino
Design and artwork production: Arco da Velha
Typesetting: Paulo Resende
Print and Binding: Cafilesa

ISBN: 978-989-655-197-1

Legal Deposit: 373935/14

Contents

FROM PETER DRUCKER,
THE FOUNDER OF MODERN MANAGEMENT,
TO MOURINHO,
THE LEADER PRACTITIONER

I do not know if Mourinho ever read anything written by Drucker (1909-2005), by far the most quoted management thinker.

But he surely, at least intuitively, exemplifies much of what Drucker used to teach in his classes. Both regarding **professional development** and on being a **manager**.

"What are you good at, what are your strength(s)?", would Drucker ask looking straight into our eyes.

And when the student mumbled he would cut him short and say: *"shame on you."*

"No, no" – he would insist, not a shopping list or a hero sandwich, but one, just **one thing** that you excell at.

The old maxim of Gnôthi Seauton (know thyself) in the front of the Delphos temple in ancient Greece was such an obsession of Drucker, that he became known in Mexico as *"el señor una cosa"*.

But then Drucker would explain: *"you see, if you (1ˢᵗ) find the one thing you excell at and (then) select a job where that thing is very, very important, you may have all the weaknesses in the world, that they do not matter, they become irrelevant, as they are not critical, key success factors, to do the job well".*

Thus one should forget about developing our weaknesses and focus on building on our strengths. You have *empathy*. You will become a great *salesman/woman* as that is the number one quality that one must have in order to sell, according to Jack Welch former president of General Electric and considered the best world manager in the last quarter of the 20th century.

You are a *contrarian*? Your place is in **staff** playing devil's advocate (what the late Kirby Warren called *contention management*) to all kinds of plans which reach headquarters to spend money: a new advertising campaign, the acquisition of a new generation of machinery, or the enlargement of the warehouse, whatsoever. Alfred Sloan, who recovered General Motors from near bankruptcy into the dominant automobile corporation in the world, never, never took any decision without having knowledge of both sides of the question in hand. He would simply postpone the decision.

Still, it does not matter your looks, neither your ignorance, neither still your lack of skills (in writing, reading, etc.), if you have (1) a good voice, (2) sympathy and (3) you execute routine tasks fast, that's all it takes to be a great *phone operator*.

"Do you know what's the secret in life?", asked Jack Palance to Billy Crystal in the movie City Slickers. Only then to answer: *"One thing, just one thing and the rest does not matter. What's that one thing? That's what you have to find for yourself"*.

And that's the first secret of Mourinho's success[1]. He is not a superman with only a wide range of qualities. Some kind of renaissance man.

At school he never excelled in various subjects including mathematics. At university he gave up on a business degree. And later on – much to his regret – he tried but abandoned being a professional football player: he was simply not good enough.

---

1   And the role of a great teacher, one must add. As Benjamin Disraeli once noted "the greatest good you can do for another, is not just to share your riches, but to reveal to him his own." For such a purpose both S. Ignatius of Loyola and Calvin stressed the feedback method. Anyway to know one-self is no easy task, for sure. As Wittgenstein pointed out the easiest thing in life is to deceive ourselves. Self knowledge requires the hard work of thinking (Bernard Shaw noted that most people think once, twice a year and that he made a living thinking once a week) and courage (which Churchill called the supreme quality) to see in the crudest terms our weaknesses, what we are not good at, rather than engaging in wishful thinking and self-deception.

Those interested in the topic may find useful to check: Shakespeare, Henry V and the lessons for management; J. A. Vasconcellos e Sá; Vida Económica; 2010.

But while most start considering a career as a coach, around 34/35 years of age, Mourinho at 15 years old was already receiving money for observing opposing teams (in professional leagues) and in helping in transmitting messages to the players in the field. Thus at twenty when studying for his university degree in physical education, one of his most senior professors (Manuel Sergio) commented that *"Mourinho already knew more about football than, I myself"*. A little later he was acting as a translator to Bobby Robson and preparing to become a coach.

And then of course, Mourinho followed the discovery of *"his one thing"* with the upmost **concentration** and dedication.

When he received his first invitation to be head coach (at Benfica), he left home and went to a hotel room spending a few days preparing in absolute isolation. Next at Oporto he initially lived at the football academy. Usually, he arrives 1h30m before the start of the training sessions: to check the grass, the equipments, etc. to see if everything is in order.

"After the games", says his wife Matilde *"we usually go out for dinner. At the beginning he starts by asking how was my day and that of the children. At the middle of the meal he starts slowly speaking about football. And at dessert he grasps a piece of paper and begins telling me what will be the team for the next game and what will its tactics be. That's how he is and that's how he will always be"*.

Much in the way of Drucker who when once chitchatting with students at the end of a class was asked what were his hobbies in free time only to answer: *"what free time?"*. And offered Verdi and Phidias as examples.

While watching a performance of the composer's last opera in Hamburg, Drucker learned that his last opera, Falstaff, had been written when he was eighty, reflecting Verdi's philosophy that *"all my life I have strived for perfection. Although it always eluded we surely have an obligation to make one more try"*.

Phidias was the sculptor in charge of the statues at the Parthenon temple in Athens. As he was going about his work he was questioned why he was working scrupulously on the back of the statues as they would be turned to the columns sustaining the temple and thus no one would see them. "*The gods will*", was his answer.

Mourinho is, says Vitor Baia, (the former goalkeeper of Oporto and the Portuguese selection), "*completely dedicated to his job and passionate about his work. That's one of his most intrinsic qualities. Thus it is only too natural that he is always working, programming and anticipating.*"

"*To be one step ahead*", agrees Didier Drogba "*is paramount to Mourinho. He prepares before a game start for various scenarios, regardless of who is the next opposing team playing: he shows us videos, how the other team plays, its best player(s), strengths and weaknesses, everything to the smallest detail. For him there are no easy games, but only respect for the next adversary, whoever it may be*".

The point here is **not** that one must be a workaholic in order to succeed. But simply that one **must first** find what one is very good at: the one thing where one excells. And **then** focus on it obsessively: The rest? Means nothing. First things first, second things never (Drucker). Focus? It stands for: follow on course until success.

And **finally** if the one thing, the sole which matters, is also something you like, so much better. Not only what you do will come naturally and performance easy, but it will also be pleasurable: when we love what we do, we will never work one single day in our life.

Thus: find the "one thing", focus there; and enjoy it.

But if building on strengths (rather than trying to improve weaknesses), applies to all kinds and sorts of professions, there is another Drucker's advice (again exemplified by Mourinho) which is specific to leadership.

Let us step back for a minute. There are **three types of people in life**: amateurs which produce nothing but excuses. Professionals which produce results by themselves. And leaders which produce results *through others*.

It is so that most of the definitions of a leader center around making others achieving objectives.

But to accomplish that there are **two things** a leader must do.

The first is to be a **manager**. Forget about charisma, power, acting as a Sancho Panza, a confederate cavalry officer, whatever.

Some temperamental characteristics (fortitude, character) help, but mostly and foremost a leader must manage: set objectives, organize, communicate (well), motivate and control. How can anyone attain objectives through others without managing?

Second, in order to excell as a manager, the leader must use the **inverted pyramid**.

In corporations that means putting the client at the top (since only clients can guarantee jobs – Jack Welch – and thus the client is the boss – P. Kotler). Then in the second line are those in constant contact with the clients: the sales force, people at the branches, etc. Next, below, come the supervisors, who help the above (front)line serve the clients. And as the inverted pyramid narrows down with fewer and fewer people on each line, come the middle managers, then the top managers and finally at the bottom of the inverted pyramid is the CEO, the company president[2].

Thus the **manager (leader)** is not at the top, but **at the bottom of the inverted pyramid**. Not ahead of his/her followers, but behind, pointing the direction (*"for me* (Mourinho) *to lead is not to give orders, but to guide"*), pushing, acting as a facilitator (coordinating, solving conflicts and optimizing working conditions) and finally controlling and intervening only when occur deviations from the preset course or mistakes.

The leader (manager) is a shepherd (of the tribe into the promised land). God through Jesus said: Peter, shepherd my flock. In short, he acts as an older brother precisely what Ferran Soriano[3], (vice-president of the Barcelona management team which took the club from a constant loser to the world top), observed in the behavior of great coaches: F. Rijkaard, P. Guardiola and of course, Mourinho.

A coach also has a client: the **club he works for**, in the words of Mourinho: *"we (the coaches and players) are the microstructure serving the macrostructure: the club's president, the investors and the supporters"*.

---

2 Those interested in how to manage the inverted pyramid can check: There is no leadership, only effective management; J.A. Vasconcellos e Sá; Vida Económica, 2012.

3 The ball does not go in by chance, Ferran Soriano, Palgrave Macmillan, November 2011.

And he can serve that client, only through **victories** (that's the only way to serve the client's needs) and there you have the start of Mourinho managing the inverted pyramid: *"you are great players, but so far you have won nothing, zero, nill"*, was Mourinho's very first talk to the players when he arrived at Chelsea for the first time; *"Mourinho gave us thirst for victories, the rage for victories"* (Galles, Kelly); *"since the first day he only thinks and talks about victories, regardless if we are going to play with Manchester, Barcelona, whoever, his only thought is always victory"* (Jorge Costa).

Then follows the rest, the other requirements to manage the inverted (by opposition to the traditional) pyramid. Besides putting the client at the top.

First **decentralization/participati**on: *"Mourinho provokes dialogues, discussions to discover what is in our mind and decides together with all"* (Vitor Baia); *"Mourinho asks our opinions without ever losing sight of his owns, or fearing for loss of authority"* (Jorge Costa).

Next **motivati**on: *"he makes us not only feel we can win, but makes us absolutely convinced of that: that we are the best"* (J. Costa, again); *"he changed us in such a way that no one can imagine ... before we were normal players, now we are warriors which fight for each other ... he infected us with the virus of victory"* (Drogba).

To be followed by the clearest possible **communica**tion, which means first of all to recognize that genuine communication, to get the message across, depends mostly on the ears of the receiver and not the mouth of the sender. People receive and process information based on their experience and according to what they are (*"we see things <u>not</u> as they are, but as we are"* – Anaïs Nin).

Jesus spoke by parables. And Socrates recommended: when speaking to a carpenter use carpentry examples.

Thus *"he starts by knowing very well the individual personality of each player, how best to communicate and make the psychological management of him"* (Deco).

"I am distant and close. Can be very far away or intimate. I am everything. It depends upon the situation and the player. Some players I never, ever, embrace because they do not feel the need. With others I act as a paternal figure. I analyze case by case, moment by moment,

personality by personality, and act accordingly. The relation? Not an end by itself, my aim is not to be friendly, or liked, but solely to contribute to the team's performance, that's all" (Mourinho).

And finally **organization/coordination** (*"he does not teach us how to play football, but how to play together as a team, which is quite different"* – Drogba), and **discipl**ine, through **control** and **intervention** when (but only when) the player's responsibility fails. Sabry, Sousa, Postiga, Baia, Deco, McCarthy, Maniche, they all are life examples that there are no stars, only work and that no one is greater than the group: *"when part of a group, we do not exist alone by ourselves and the whole can never be sacrificed for the individual; on the contrary I sacrifice the individual for the collective"* (Mourinho).

In short, the inverted pyramid requires that a culture of **responsibility** permeates the group from top to the lower levels, players and non players alike. When playing against Blackburn, Tiago was replaced and Chelsea's physiotherapist Mike Bank had forgotten to bring into the bench the needed water, vitamins, coats, blankets, etc… in a few seconds Mourinho turned to him and you could see Bank running as crazy through the tunnel to get everything that was missing.

"The buck may well stop with the leader" (Truman), but as the late Steve Jobs remembered everyday and everybody working with him: *"the group expects each one to do his duty".*

But, much, much better than I, Luis Lourenço explains how Mourinho manages the inverted pyramid with the clients (the supporters, the investors, the president, the group) at the top, and the leader (at the bottom), by setting goals, communicating well, organizing, coordinating, motivating, controlling and intervening only, but only, when needed. Thus supplying the product (that his clients crave for): victories.

And that is why we must be very **grateful to all three**. First to **Drucker** for brilliantly stressing the important. Then to **Mourinho** for exemplifying it in practice (*and action is the best eloquence* – L. da Vinci). And finally to **Lourenço** for systematizing everything in the simplest possible way.

What of course, is extremely hard and difficult to achieve. In life what is simple is to complicate; what is complicated is to simplify.

Thus as the great architect Constantin Brancusi stressed *simplicity is complexity solved*. And Lourenço achieved just that.

So, if you want to **enjoy in the clearest possible terms the secrets of Mourinho's succes**s, all you have to do is just turn to the next page. Good reading.

JORGE A. VASCONCELLOS E SÁ
PROFESSOR AT U.T./AESE/IESE / SWISS BUSINESS SCHOOL /
INTERNATIONAL BUSINESS SCHOOL OF SCANDINAVIA /
HULT INTERNATIONAL BUSINESS SCHOOL LONDON

1. THE LEADER THINKS AHEAD

On the bench, I heard him describe what would happen with nearly surgical precision. It was almost disquieting, at times. It was as if he could see the future. DIDIER DROGBA

May 6th, 2007 was, curiously, a beautiful day in the English capital. The sun shone down on the Emirates Stadium, the brand new Arsenal stadium where Chelsea would play and where nothing but victory was acceptable. If they didn't win, they would relinquish the Premier League title to Manchester United.

After three years in England, life had never been so difficult for José Mourinho, Chelsea's manager. In England, always at the service of the Blues[1], he had won five trophies, including two Premiership titles, as many as he had disputed. At the third attempt, retaining the title was beginning to look like a mirage. In order to win it, Chelsea had to win their two remaining matches, and had to hope that Manchester United would lose at least one match. A penalty and the subsequent dismissal of a disoriented Boulahrouz[2] in the first half heralded a bad ending for that wonderful sunny day. In the second half, Chelsea managed to equalize, but that was all it amounted to: a draw. The Premier League went straight to Sir Alex Ferguson's Manchester United. Defeat had caught up with Mourinho.

Until that May 6, 2007 the question had buzzed in my ears time and time again; I would even say that I had been asked about it thousands of times. The people who knew about my close relationship with José Mourinho had always been curious to see how Mourinho

---

[1] Nickname given to the Chelsea FC team, due to their blue kit.

[2] Dutch international player signed by Chelsea in that season. At the end of the season, he would leave the team due to poor performances throughout the year.

would face defeat. The question "how will Mourinho react in defeat?" was pertinent, and I had also wondered how his reaction would be. After all, José Mourinho is the "Special One[3]" and, at least apparently, "Special Ones" are not expected to lose.

Besides, Mourinho had never really lost, so defeat would be something new in his life. For someone who had won so often, how would not winning feel? His temper, his nature if you will, wasn't exactly in his favour. Mourinho had always won and always made a point to underline that fact, an attitude that creates a lot of envy – winning alone does – and hatred. Thus, lots of people were waiting to rub their hands with glee at the first loss of the man who had never lost; how would he react to his players, his followers, his fans, since none of them knew the taste of defeat with Mourinho? Many more reasons could be named here to justify the almost universal curiosity – even from those who idolize him – of how Mourinho would react in defeat. I'll say it again: I was aware that the "Special One" would lose eventually, so I would muse on how his reaction would be at that bitter first defeat. At one point, I could not resist and – I don't know if he remembers this – I asked him how it would be. "*Normal*" – he replied – "*It will be like with everyone else. I know I will lose one day and I'm prepared for it, so I don't even think about it. I know it's going to happen, period. When it happens I'll be here to face the consequences that a defeat always brings. However, I don't think it will be anything special in terms of attitude or reaction.*" I don't recall very well, but I had to wait another two or three years, at least, to learn how it would really be.

While writing these words, I review the images on Sporttv[4] that I recorded on that sunny afternoon of May 6, 2007. The time is exactly 8 seconds before the end of the match. The cameras are already set on a heartbroken Essien, down on his knees, exhausted by the effort, frowning, foreseeing the inevitable. Essien was the perfect image of

---

[3] The nickname by which José Mourinho is known worldwide. It was given to him by British journalists after his first press conference in England. Mourinho said that he considered himself a special coach after winning the UEFA Cup and the Champions League in consecutive seasons.

[4] Portuguese television channel

defeat and the English director made sure to show it to the world. When the final whistle was blown, José Nunes, the Portuguese journalist from the TV station, says: "*The* Premier League *goes to Manchester United, the new English champions!*", while the English cameras are already focusing on José Mourinho. Finally, it was time to show the world the reaction of the "Special One", *José's*, at the exact moment of defeat. What many thought would be Mourinho's last secret, would finally be revealed to the world. But proceeding the match description on television, we can see Mourinho's immediate reaction, still on the bench, at the final whistle, hugging two of his assistants, a cold almost mechanical hug, with heedless eyes, revealing the ideas now whirling in his head. Would they? Then, we see Mourinho going onto the pitch with a firm step and the television cameras focus on other actors: Essien, who maintained the same heartbroken expression, lost really, wiped the sweat from his brow with his shirt; Kalou lies down on the pitch and contemplates the sky until someone comes to lift him up; captain John Terry bends over, his hands on his knees, and thoughtfully observes the sunlit grass that still shines brightly. These images inspire the journalist from Sporttv, who comments: "*... but Chelsea are still standing, showing great professionalism, great attitude and great character here on Arsenal's pitch.*" The picture changes again and we see José Mourinho walking, steadfast and hasty, on the pitch of the Emirates Stadium. He walks by Jens Lehmann, the opposing goalkeeper, and without stopping, without even breaking stride, shakes his hand. Where will he go after defeat? What will he do in that hasty and determined way?

When he shakes Lehmann's hand, the journalist begins to anticipate what, for me, would be one of the most fantastic and intense manifestations of José Mourinho's leadership: "*... it is noteworthy the way Mourinho greets his teammates and opponents, leaving this match with dignity...*" And it's precisely when these words are uttered, that we see Mourinho, who keeps walking and gazing at the stands for the Chelsea fans, pointing his arm firmly stretched, even stiff, I would say, at his players. He points, looks at the fans, turns his face, and while still pointing, looks at his players. The footage is extraordinary with the camera lost in a wonderful ballet around the "man of the hour", but certainly, not for the reasons he and *Blues* fans wished. The picture changes again and now, just a split second later, José Mourinho has a new camera behind him, filming him from the back, small, tiny, an insignificant dot against the huge background of Chelsea fans standing in front of him completely filling the stands of the Arsenal stadium, as far as the eye can see. Yet, this small image of the man only further highlights the magnitude and impact of his gesture. At this time, Mourinho takes his left hand to his chin, raises his head slightly up, to the point of having to look down to be able to look at the crowd.

Arsenal-Chelsea (1-1) May 5, 2007.
The tie gave the title to Man Utd.
Head on.

Chelsea-Man Utd (1-0) May 19, 2007.
Chelsea won the FA Cup. Players
celebrate. Head on.

His hand is outstretched and he touches his chin slightly with the back of his hand, and then realization came. In defeat, Mourinho did nothing more than reunite his tribe; a tribe that had lost, yes, but with their heads held high, and therefore deserves full applause. That is precisely the meaning of his gesture. Chelsea's players had lost, it's true, but they had lost with their heads held high, they fell as the champions they were, and that deserves a round of applause. I was watching these images in Setúbal, Mourinho's birthplace in Portugal, and I immediately decoded them. Some gestures are universal. At the "Emirates", English Chelsea fans also got the message, and immediately erupted into applause to the champions who had ceased to be. After all, this was what Mourinho wanted: to honour his players in defeat. And so, at this time, we can hear the commentator Joaquim Rita saying: "*This is an example of the great leader, who tried everything to avoid defeat. He failed... Chelsea was fantastic, especially in the second half... as the saying goes: trees die standing and so do great champions. This is what I get from Chelsea.*" At this precise moment, the image shows the strong, heartfelt and complicit hug between José Mourinho and the vice-captain Frank Lampard. By now, most of Chelsea's players were next to Mourinho, thanking the unremitting cheering of their supporters. Then, Mourinho hugs Lampard and, at the same time, stretches his arm out to Terry, the captain. It's the moment of embrace among the three leaders of the operational Chelsea, of the field Chelsea on the ground, of the Chelsea that can smell the grass, of the Chelsea that wins and loses on the pitch: coach and captains. An image that obviously doesn't go unnoticed by the commentator: "*... here we see the two leaders, Lampard and Terry, hugging Mourinho,*" and also to the journalist who leads the comment, and complements Joaquim Rita's words: "*... there it is, quite outstanding images indeed, and they will surely be seen around the world on this day, when Chelsea hands the League title to Manchester United.*" By now, the images show half-naked Chelsea players, wearing only their shorts, since their shirts, and even captain John Terry's armband, were sent to the stands as a thank you for their fans' support. As for the fans: some are crying, something the television report emphasizes, and nobody gets tired of applauding... in defeat. And what, in many cases, would be a time of silence, of arms down, of disappointment, became a celebration after all and, perhaps more importantly, a kind of projection of the celebration that would follow at the brand new Wembley Stadium two weeks later – when Chelsea would face the new champions Manchester United in a mouth-watering FA Cup final. At that time, in Setúbal, sitting alone on my couch, sad for my friend's defeat, I smiled slightly and said to myself: "*I know you too well. The championship is a thing of the past, it's not important anymore. You're already preparing the next match, preparing the final. This tribute you are paying to the players is nothing but a preparation for the match against Manchester United for their motivation and self-esteem. Unquestionably, the FA Cup final has already begun, at least for Chelsea...*"

José Mourinho lost the Premier League there, but it would have been the same if he had won. The moment is only worth the split second when it is happening. The present moment is just something that is constantly passing. In each present moment, the future is all that matters and thus it is lived, and it's the projection of such future that makes us who we are. José Mourinho is, therefore, a predator of victories, but only future ones. So, as paradoxical as it sounds, both wins and defeats are not that important. The only thing that matters is what has not been achieved yet. Still sitting on my couch, with the players and staff of both Chelsea and Arsenal now in the dressing room, I found myself going back in time, about two years earlier, to June 2005.

After eleven years, Benfica had finally won the Portuguese title. The manager, Giovanni Trapattoni, was an Italian in his 60s and, therefore, highly experienced. For Benfica, undoubtedly the greatest Portuguese club, two consecutive years without winning is a tragedy for their fans – which amount to a few million – let alone eleven years. Imagine that! It was "only" the longest period in the history of the club without winning the title. It was natural that the celebration among the supporters of the club was a blast. But would this also be natural among the players and the managers? If the club had nothing more to win that season, it certainly would, however, that was not the case. Benfica was crowned national champion, and eight days later had a match with Vitória de Setúbal at Estádio do Jamor to compete in the Portuguese Cup. At that time, I was the director for Vitória Futebol Clube/SAD. Within the club we were all aware of the scale of the problem that was to win against Benfica. We had, in fact, full notion that "their" team was better than "ours", but since there is no such thing as early winners in football or in life, we were doing everything to counter Benfica's favouritism. That's why we decided to train the team in a football training facility in the centre of the country, during the week leading up to the match. While we worked and rested, we watched Benfica celebrating all week long. Directors, technical staff and players strolled and celebrated the title they had won the weekend before. There were parties almost every day until Wednesday or Thursday; even on early Friday morning two or three Benfica players were caught celebrating in nightclubs. The end result was a 2-1 defeat for Benfica. A fair defeat that no one challenged, given that Benfica's players did little to win. I thought back to Mourinho to conclude that none of this would have ever happened with him. Never. Why not? Because Mourinho always thinks about the future. In Benfica's case, they were only thinking and celebrating the past, without looking to the future. No one noticed it and no one cared. If they had planned for the future, they could have celebrated two victories instead of just one. While comparing Benfica, at the time of its first win after eleven years, with José Mourinho, at the time of his first ever loss, I understood Mourinho's answer to all of those, including myself, who had wondered how his first moment of defeat would be. He reacted like a great champion and above all a great leader. He reacted by preparing the victory two weeks later in the FA Cup final; he started rehabilitating his players right there, uniting his fans, strengthening the ties of the group and consolidating his leadership. I think most people understood this, so much so that even among his detractors, there was not a lot of rejoicing, because they recognized the greatness of Mourinho's moment as a man, as a coach and as a leader. Many wept a hopeless defeat, while Mourinho was already thinking and preparing the next challenge, the next victory.

Actually, it is not difficult to understand why. A leader, whoever he might be, is only one while focusing on the future. As I said earlier, that future is lived from the excitement of the present moment, the only ontologically effective instance. Why? Because the leader is the one who has already seen what others have not; the one that, in some way, has been in the future, has had the vision, the perception of what will happen and the right path to take. He is the one that has already "seen the movie in his mind", as António Damásio[5] would say.

I can not resist transcribing the words of Didier Drogba, the Ivory Coast international, and Mourinho's player at Chelsea, in an interview reported by the newspaper Correio da Manhã on May 26, 2008: *"On the bench, I heard him describe what would happen with nearly surgical precision. It was almost disquieting, at times. It was as if he could see the future."*

When I interviewed Didier Drogba for this book in March 2010, I asked him to give me an example that illustrated his statement:

---

[5] Famous Portuguese neuroscientist, who has lived in the U.S. for 30 years. He develops his work in the area of neurobiology, human behavior and as a researcher of the areas of the brain responsible for decision making and conduct.

I can recall the first time we went to Barcelona, to play in the Champions League in the 2004-05 season. It was the first qualifying round and we still had to play the second leg in England. In that game I was penalized with a red card, and I thought the referee was wrong. In the end, he was especially harsh to the referee and criticized him hard. At the end of the press conference, he returned to our dressing rooms and told us he had spoken to the journalists condemning the referee. Then he added: 'And you will see, when we get to Stamford Bridge, Collina will referee the match (Pierluigi Collina is still considered the best referee ever). You'll see, it's a given'.

And who was the referee in England? You can go and check: Collina! Amazing!!!

Can we say that Mourinho is one step ahead?

We can say that at least he tries to. This is his constant exercise, and he gets it most of the times. See, when a football match starts, you need to think fast and be prepared for two scenarios: the bad one and the good one. When we can anticipate them and know how to act before either one, it's easier to understand and play the game. An example of what I have just said is Mourinho's preparation for the FA Cup matches (with inferior teams). He prepares them in the same way as if we were playing against a team from the Premier League. He shows us videos, so that we can see how the team plays, which one is the best player, what are the team's strengths and weaknesses, everything down to the smallest detail. There are no easy matches for him, and we always have to respect our opponent, whichever it is. This is a fantastic attitude.

Taking advantage of this idea of "getting ahead", it would be interesting to find out how people in general see José Mourinho as a public figure. Will Mourinho be regarded by most people as a manager – his profession – or as a leader, a status resulting from his profession, but perhaps no less important from the way he carries out his work?

I have no doubt that he is seen as a football coach in the world of football, after all, what he intrinsically is.

However, the question facing us here has another framework. It is a matter of much larger scope; what interests us now is to try to understand, taking advantage of the global media profile which

Mourinho enjoys, how the vast majority of people scattered around the world see him: as a football coach, or as a leading influencer of people. Only if and when the latter is confirmed, will it be possible to learn the lessons needed for what is intended here: the transfer of a certain 'Mourinho's way' to the organizational world in general. Therefore, for a better understanding of the subject, I think it's interesting to watch the advertising campaign of American Express, which chose José Mourinho as the company's face to the world, except the US, which, as we know, has little interest in football[6]. First, one should consider the type of product that AMEX sells – credit cards – and therefore the target audience you want to reach – the middle class/ upper middle class. For this type of product, Mourinho was chosen to pass a certain message. However, the marketing department at AMEX did not choose the image of Mourinho as a football coach, the man on the bench leading his team, or training, or in any of the activities carried out by a manager. Instead, they created a very different picture using several adverts illustrative of the message they wished to pass on, the message that José Mourinho naturally conveys. Which message is it? Let me describe the different adverts.

In one advert, Mourinho enters his car and drives out of his garden in reverse; the front gate is already open. Suddenly, Mourinho hits the breaks and the Jeep stops. The viewer wonders why. He remains still, looking back, when suddenly you see a ball outside the gate, then a child running after the ball, and then a lady running after the child. Conclusion: José Mourinho is one step ahead; it is difficult to catch him off guard.

In another advert, Mourinho drops his son off at school. He leaves the child there and opens his umbrella, while still on the school grounds. A few seconds later there is a thunderstorm. People run for shelter because nobody else has an umbrella. The weather never bothers Mourinho, who walks peacefully under his umbrella. Conclusion: Mourinho foresaw what no one else did; Mourinho is one step ahead.

---

[6] Out of curiosity, it is interesting that the U.S. celebrity chosen to replace José Mourinho in the AMEX's promotional campaign was the famous actor Robert de Niro.

In a third advert, Mourinho is in the hallway leading to his office when he collides with an employee who has a cup of coffee in his hand. Mourinho's shirt is ruined due to the size of the coffee stain. The employee apologizes profusely. Mourinho says there is no problem. In the next image we see Mourinho entering his office, going to a closet and taking an identical shirt, just for this kind of emergency. Conclusion: Mourinho does not let life surprise him; Mourinho predicts and anticipates life's contingencies.

In yet another advert, the only one that has to do with football, we see Mourinho explaining how he wants a set piece to be taken by his players. The following image shows the match where you see a player hit a corner. Then, the camera shows Mourinho, peaceful on the bench, with thousands of fans behind him enthusiastically celebrating the goal that resulted from that corner kick. Mourinho does not even blink, because he knew that, if the players did what he had told them, a goal would be the natural result. Conclusion: Mourinho is competent, he explains how to do it, and if the players follow his lead, they will get fantastic results.

In a final advert, an alleged daughter of Mourinho scribbles on a sheet of paper on the kitchen table, waiting for the toast to "pop-up" out of the toaster. Mourinho comes into the kitchen at the exact moment the toast is ejected into the air. He catches it, effortlessly. He puts the toast on the plate beside him, gives it to the girl and continues on his way towards the kitchen door. Conclusion: even in simple moments, Mourinho naturally thinks ahead.

The icing on the cake of this commercial always comes at the end of each advert with the words uttered by José Mourinho: *"My life is about keeping one step ahead. That's why my card is American Express."* Of course, none of this is innocent. The creatives at AMEX know exactly which markets to exploit, what kind of promotional vehicle they have on their hands and how to reach its target audience. Mourinho as a coach? No! Mourinho as a leader, and the image of that leadership is passed on to us in different ways and in different environments, but always with a common denominator: Mourinho anticipates, sees what others do not see. Therefore, I cannot find a stronger, more powerful image of today's leadership than this one – someone who has seen the way before any other. Leadership means to command, to lead, to guide people through unknown paths. Nowadays, with the constant change in our lives that's what leadership means. Change takes us into the unknown, into uncertainty; the leader leads us, guides us through this unknown and uncertain path, because he has already been there somehow (visionary), he has already seen this way and knows where to go. Obviously, leadership is not confined to this concept alone, but it sure has a lot of it. Change makes us uncomfortable because it is, and suggests to us, the uncertain, the unknown. Hence, we need someone to guide us on this uncomfortable and unknown path. Since change is here to stay, so are the leaders, and with them, the increasingly sharp debate around this topic.

Consequently, it is understandable that leaders end up being a little like our heroes, the everyday flesh and blood heroes, present, tangible; thus, not only do they lead us, they also inspire and awaken the best in us and make us dream. As William Shakespeare said through Prospero, the protagonist of *The Tempest*: "*We are such stuff / As dreams are made on*". Who wouldn't want to be a little like Mourinho? The successful man, competent, fearless, brave and good-looking. After all, who would not want to be Mourinho, the romantic hero of our time? This is the image that is shown by the marketing department of another prominent multinational corporation: SAMSUNG. In the images that were seen worldwide, we can see Mourinho using a parachute to dive from a helicopter, rappelling from a window to the ground or jumping from the roof of a building to another, and finally enter, impeccably dressed, in suit and tie, inside the meeting room of a top executive. Mourinho is compared to none other than James Bond, the famous secret agent on Her Majesty's Service. Mourinho is like 007, the romantic hero of our times. His courage, ability to make decisions under stress, self-sacrifice, intelligence, competence, etc., he's the man who makes us dream, that we all tend to mimic a little, because Bond is another hero, another leader of our time influencing crowds at various levels. Bond ... James Bond, is also one who anticipates, who foresees and who is never surprised, otherwise he'd be dead by now, with the forces of evil winning the "terrible battle" against the forces of good, of which 007 is its most illustrious representative and defender.

It seems clear that José Mourinho is not just seen as just a football coach these days. Today, his media figure has long surpassed that barrier. José Mourinho moves crowds who want to see him wherever he goes. He influences thousands of young people and adults, not only for his "unkempt" way of being, but also for his "careless" appearance – of which his five o'clock shadow beard is perhaps his greatest icon – and companies would like him to publicize their brands. Definitely, nowadays José Mourinho is not just a football coach. That is why he is an idol, a world-famous leader.

What kind of leader are we talking about? What kind of leader is this one that became the global public figure he is today, in just four or five years? What kind of leader is this that became successful in so little time and leads his followers to achieve absolutely extraordinary things, perhaps beyond their own worth? What kind of leader is this whom Manuel Sérgio[7] referred to as a "new kind of coach for a new kind of football" (Sérgio, 2003: Preface), and that when he left English football got a written note – absolutely unprecedented fact – from the British Prime Minister Gordon Brown to the press, where he admitted: *"José Mourinho has made a significant contribution to British football in a short period of time and he's also one of the great characters of the game"*, amongst many other things that could be quoted here.

PA SNAP: 11.39, 20/09/07 Prime Minister Gordon Brown:
"Jose Mourinho has made a significant contribution to British football in a short period of time and he's also one of the great characters of the game."

Clearly José Mourinho is a different kind of leader, who speaks and acts differently. These differences were evident early in his career, not only for what he suddenly achieved, but also due to the way he behaved with his followers, with the reporters, finally, as he asserted himself in a profession, working for highly mediatised clubs. Just look at the table of his major victories:

[7] Sports Philosopher and former professor of Mourinho.

HEAD COACH

2013-14   **CHELSEA**

2012-13   **REAL MADRID**
Spanish Super Cup
IFFHS World's Best Club Coach

2011-12   **REAL MADRID**
Spanish League (La Liga)

2010-11   **REAL MADRID**
Spanish Cup
FIFA Coach of the Year
IFFHS World's Best Club Coach

2009-10   **INTER**
UEFA Champions League
Italian League (Serie A)
Italian Cup

2008-09   **INTER**
Italian League (Serie A)
Italian Super Cup

2006-07   **CHELSEA**
FA Cup
League Cup (Carling Cup)

2005-06   **CHELSEA**
Premier League
Super Cup
UEFA Manager of the Year
IFFHS World's Best Club Coach

2004-05   **CHELSEA**
Premier League
League Cup (Carling Cup)
UEFA Manager of the Year
IFFHS World's Best Club Coach

2003-04   **FC PORTO**
UEFA Champions League
Portuguese League
Portuguese Super Cup

2002-03   **FC PORTO**
UEFA Cup
Portuguese League
Portuguese Cup

2001-02   **UNIÃO DE LEIRIA** (6 months) and **FC PORTO** (5 months)

2000-01   **BENFICA** (2 months)

BEFORE BEING HEAD COACH

Junior manager at Vitória de Setúbal

Estrela da Amadora, assistant manager to Manuel Fernandes

Sporting Lisbon, assistant manager to Bobby Robson
Porto, assistant manager to Bobby Robson
Barcelona, assistant manager to Bobby Robson
Barcelona, assistant manager to Louis Van-Gaal

Finally, let us see how Mourinho himself thinks others see him:

On a global level, including people with different cultural backgrounds other than only football people, I think they see me more as a leader, as a human resources manager, someone who can pull off a good performance from the people I work with, someone who achieves results in a particular area – in this case football – but who could also get results in any other area, taking into account the characteristics of leadership.

Regarding the world of football, if we ask, today, the vast majority of players who have worked with me, which moments they remember, the moments that made the biggest impression on them, I believe they won't say this or that replacement in a certain match, or in victory X the Y decision made. More than any technical aspect of my decisions, which truly made an impression on them, what they really remember were the characteristics of my personality, if you will, the characteristics of my leadership, how I led the group, how I made an impression on them on a human level. This is what I think, without ever having asked, this type of question to anyone, namely to any player who has ever worked with me in the past.

2. THE PARADIGM
OF COMPLEXITY

"We don't see things as they are, we see them as we are."
(ANAÏS NIN, FRENCH NOVELIST, 1902-1977)

We begin this chapter with an example of how José Mourinho disciplines his teams. It is a case study, just an example, but it illustrates a certain way of seeing football, things, life and the world. For now, it probably won't be easy for the reader to understand these words through the example that I will transcribe ahead. Most likely, you are wondering what any of this has to do with the perspective of complexity. It is natural, do not worry or feel uncomfortable. Through this chapter, you will be able to understand José Mourinho's words about how, in a particular case, to discipline a team when signs of indiscipline begin to appear.

At the end of the 2002/03 season, after FC Porto won everything, meaning, the Portuguese League, the Portuguese Cup and the UEFA Cup, Mourinho feared a change of attitude from his players:

Following the success of the first season, where we won all there was to win, I 'was afraid' of the second [season]. I 'feared' the players' approach to the season, especially on a mental and psychological level, on a motivational level, their behaviour, their development (good or bad), some players' status... And my main concern about how to keep the group 'under control' was to 'expand' my model, make it evolve into a more rigorous game model.

In the first season it was necessary to make a statement through the quality of play. Not only the result was important but the quality of play as well. There was no need for that in the second season, and I chose control within the group through rigidity and playing discipline. I 'feared' that the status we had gained, might lead some players to misinterpret the freedom they had on the pitch. And the truth is that, during the preparatory period, I could see signs that pointed in that direction. For example, in Germany, I had to replace Maniche after 20 minutes... So I could notice a certain kind of behaviour that led me to think that it was better 'to get them on a short leash'. It wasn't fear that they would go to bed late or would drink too much; it was within the game itself.

Thus I decided that the discipline that had characterized us in the first season, within that game standard, could not be lost and the tactical rigour should increase. I knew that for the national championship, either option would be enough to win easily: my 1x4x3x3 or my 1x4x4x2. I took advantage of its greatest rigour in terms of tactical discipline, in terms of positions and roles, to work more on the 1x4x4x2[86], since this formation, the way I conceive it, is much more tactical than the 1x4x3x3[97]. A lot more tactical! In 1x4x3x3, there is a perfectly balanced occupation of the spaces from the outset, you do not need to be very 'smart', no need to think too much... just simply let the players occupy their positions. With 1x4x4x2, you need to think much more, because the pitch is occupied in a less rational manner, there is no one unmarked... The fullbacks can attack fully, but when they do so the team loses its defensive balance... If I move the players from my diamond formation to the wings, I end up with only one player in centre midfield. If the two strikers are too mobile and constantly drop to the wings, I'm left with no one in the centre to finish. It is therefore an unbalanced system (...) a system that has disadvantages. By making my players obey this tactical formation, I 'force' them to be naturally disciplined, rigorous and focused. (MOURINHO IN OLIVEIRA ET AL 2006: 177-8)

What evidence does this example provide? For now, I'll just tell you that everything about Mourinho's work is naturally integrated. Nothing can be seen or developed separately.

Right now, I only want you to bear this idea in mind: did you notice that Mourinho's act of leadership – we are talking about

---

[8] Tactical formation used in football that reflects the arrangement of players on the pitch. In this case, the team plays with the goalkeeper, 4 defenders, 4 midfielders and 2 strikers.

[9] Here the team plays with the goalkeeper, 4 defenders, 3 midfielders and 3 strikers.

motivation, therefore leadership or leadership in action – is all contextualized in training, around a ball, with the remaining components – tactical, technical, physiological, etc., – which it is associated with?

THE PERSPECTIVE OF COMPLEXITY

Acocdirng to crurnet receasrh, the letrets of a wrod can be pacled in any odrer if the frsit and lsat letrets rtaein teihr postioin. The rmeaninig letrets can be pacled rnaodlmy, we raed the smae. The fcat is we do not raed letetr by letretr, we raed ecah wrod as a whloe.

Can you read the paragraph above? Of course you can. And yet, not a single word is correct. So why can you read it? Precisely because you read the words as a whole, not one letter at a time, gathering them only to give them meaning. The key, then, is to understand the word before spelling it. Moreover, this is one of the most natural human actions. By default, this is how we perceive everything around us from the day we are born; we see objects in their entirety before perceiving their individual parts. When we contemplate a beautiful building, a beautiful landscape, a beautiful animal, we look at the whole first and make a first analysis. We only observe the parts after that analysis. In the case of a building, for example, we absorb the whole first, which gives us a first reaction. After that, if we think it's worth it, we analyse the elements separately. It is natural that we observe the doorway, the windows, the balconies, the main stairs and so on. The whole is, therefore, our first and natural perception of the things in the world around us. However, in most cases, we do the exact opposite in our lives. Do you remember how you learned how to read and write? You didn't absorb the word as a whole, of course. You gathered the letters after you learned to recognize them separately, and gradually joined them to give them meaning. Do you remember trying to read film subtitles when you were a child? They disappeared before you managed to read the whole sentence, but after a while it stopped happening. Victory! You could finally read the whole sentence before it disappeared from the screen. You could watch translated films now. That victory came when you memorized the words as a whole, and you had no need to put the letters together to read them...

However, as I said, this is not what we want to talk about. Our reasoning, our way of being and observing is not this at all. To understand better what I have just said, we must go back in time about 4 centuries.

There we find the foundation of our thinking, the scientific method that shapes our entire way of being and acting in this world. We need to realize the paradigm of reductionist positivism that the philosopher Edgar Morin called the paradigm of simplicity or Reductionism. It is a paradigm of scientific thinking that crossed the history of Western thinking from the Seventeenth century to the present day. René Descartes gave it the primary impulse, by separating body and mind in Man. Of the development of *cogito ergo sum* (I think, therefore I am) appeared what we conventionally call the "scientific method". That statement, perhaps the most famous in the history of Philosophy, first appeared in the fourth section of the *Discourse on the Method* (1637), and suggests the idea that the foundation of existence lies in the thought or in the act of thinking. Or, if we want, through the orchestration of matter we exist separately as body and mind. With this premise, we understand the logic that separates the *res cogitans* (thinking thing) from the *res extensa* (material thing). The latter arises and can only exist and have substance through the first one. This division – mind / body – founded and developed the modern scientific method. The division, separation, hierarchy are master notions of operationalized thinking in a method that has crossed the last four centuries of Western history. From this method there developed a clear separation of the human domain, either reflecting on its nature – the role of philosophy – or focusing on the realm of matter and/or the body – the role of scientific knowledge. Philosophy and Science thus followed different and separate paths and, in doing so, they could barely avail one another, interact and cooperate, so they isolated themselves. As a result thereof, the paradigm of simplicity and its purpose is understood: its principle "either separates what is connected (disjunction) or unifies what is dispersed (reduction)" (Morin 2003:

86). Taking man as a reference, Edgar Morin leaves us an illustrative example:

Man is evidently a biological being. He is a cultural being, metabiological, who lives in a universe of language, ideas and consciousness. The paradigm of simplification requires us to separate these two realities (the biological and the cultural), and to reduce the more complex one to the less complex one. Therefore, the biological man is studied in the department of biology, as an anatomical and physiological being, etc., and the man is studied in the departments of humanities and social sciences. The brain is studied as a biological organ and the spirit, the mind, is studied as a function or psychological reality. One does not exist without the other; one is simultaneously the other, although they are treated as different terms and concepts. (MORIN 2003: 86)

From this example, where Man appears to us as a reality diversely sorted, we can state one of the major shortcomings of the reductionist thinking: it does not accept disorder. Instead, it follows the path of order forgetting that disorder is part of the universe, because only against a background of disarray can Man understand order and vice versa. Boltzman, quoted in Morin (2003), said that what we call heat is nothing more than the disorderly agitation of molecules or atoms. The reductionist paradigm sees the one and the multiple, but becomes unable to understand that the one can be multiple at the same time. Cartesianism separates and reduces the complex to the less complex possible, because it believes that by separating, isolating and knowing each and every part in detail, it will finally know the whole. After all, for this paradigm the whole is equal to the sum of the parts and nothing more.

In the twentieth century, this type of logic stopped providing answers to new problems and new issues that arose and were placed by Man. An example of this failure lies in the field of the human being and it's very close to us time- wise. I am talking about the Human Genome Project.

HUMAN GENOME AND COMPLEXITY

The scientific research project of mapping the human genome, consensually accepted as one of the most advanced enterprises in contemporary science, illustrates the limits of reductionist methods as well as the challenges facing an investigation conducted from the perspective of complexity in an interesting manner.

Thus, we can start by asking the question: what is Man? It's an ancient question and apparently, with the human genome project, we would be on the verge of knowing the answer. This project tried to give us this answer, and since we are talking about the most evolved and bold crossover between science and technology, we had hopes that the answer could indeed be obtained. Inspired primarily by the Cartesian paradigm, dividing and separating to understand the whole, the project divided Man in the lowest division that science can currently achieve: the gene. With Man genetically divided – isolated and out of context – and then sequenced, we found an answer – not *the* answer – after all, humans are more than 99.9 percent genetically alike. The reader and I are 99.9 percent genetically equal. And here is another conclusion: we are nearly identical to a mouse with a genetic difference of only 1 percent, and only after comes our proximity to a chimpanzee with a difference of 2 percent. Are we all practically the same, then? Let us forget the parts and look at the whole. The truth is, even an animal differentiates us. What does the genome project mean, then? It means that what is similar is our genetic sequence not ourselves, the individuals.

> *What all this means is that genes alone do not fully explain anything. In other words, what was discovered is that genes are like a picture of the human being, but human beings are, in their essence, a film not a photograph.* (ILHARCO 2004: 27)

After all, a film is a natural and logical sequencing of a number of photographs. As a photograph of a film that is man, the genome is only a small part of the explanation for a film with an ending still unknown.

The answer to "who we are" or "what we are" cannot be found only in our chemical, biological or genetic composition, *i.e.*, in the matter. The paper by Venter *et al* (2001) refers that due to the modest amount of human genes – rice has nearly the double of our genes... – to be able to discover the mechanisms that generate the complexities inherent to human development, and the sophisticated systems that maintain homeostasis, we must look elsewhere. That 'elsewhere' is the perspective of complexity, as the scientists themselves admit:

> *We will soon be in a position to move away from the cataloguing of individual components of the system, and beyond the simplistic notions of «this binds to that, which then docks on this, and then the complex moves there...» to the exciting area of network perturbations, nonlinear responses and thresholds, and their pivotal role in human diseases. The enumeration of the «parts lists» reveals that in organisms with complex nervous systems, neither gene number, neuron number of cell types correlates in any meaningful manner with even simplistic measures of structural or behavioural complexity.* (VENTER ET AL 2001: 1347)

The authors therefore conclude that there are fallacies in the Cartesian model of thinking that prevent us from getting at the whole from the parts, so the gene itself will never answer "who we are".

> *There are two fallacies to be avoided: determinism, the idea that all characteristics of the person are "hard-wired" by the genome; and reductionism, the view that with complete knowledge of the human genome sequence, it is only a matter of time before our understanding of gene functions and interactions will provide a complete causal description of human variability. The real challenge of human biology, beyond the task of finding out how genes orchestrate the construction and maintenance of the miraculous mechanism of our bodies, will lie ahead as we seek to explain how our minds have come to organize thoughts sufficiently well to investigate our own existence.*

(VENTER ET AL 2001: 1347)

One can understand the doubt that, against all perspectives, the project genome undid: we cannot understand Man from the parts. The answer is in the whole. Indeed, as Hegel rightly said, "the truth is the whole." The most sophisticated machines with the most advanced science cannot distinguish us (99.9% equal). How can an eight or nine month's child, a dog or a cat perfectly distinguish us? Because the human genome project looked at us with a Cartesian attitude, dividing us and studying us in parts and then looked again as a whole. A child, a dog or a cat looks at each of us, at a mouse or a building as a "whole", and it is that whole that apprehends and perceives first and primarily. Hence that look about the whole makes us so easily and dramatically different.

THE COMPLEX AND CONTEXTUALIZED WHOLE

Manuel Sérgio said: "*Mourinho is a new kind of coach.*" The "old" master knew what he was talking about. Manuel Sérgio has known Mourinho from the time he was a student and, according to Mourinho, he was perhaps the person who influenced him the most at the start of his academic and professional journey.

When I joined the Instituto Superior de Educação Física (ISEF), to graduate in Physical Education, there was a book that influenced me in a negative way – but I was forced to study it – which is seen as a 'bible' of the methodology of physical education and sport. It is a work by one Matveyev, who was – and still is – a milestone in education when it comes to individual sports. However, in my opinion, one thing is an individual sport with a man being prepared for a particular purpose and another is a team sport where one man by himself means nothing. The qualities that can be developed in individual sport with a single athlete have nothing to do with the qualities that are developed in a team sport, namely football with 11 players, and sometimes more than twenty. I disagreed completely, although I wasn't exactly the most attentive student, perhaps only minimally aware since I only wanted to graduate. I knew that my subsequent research would be much more important than that five-year university degree. I had to memorize something I did not agree with, trying to develop ideas I completely disagreed with. Matveyev's book is indeed a 'bible' for individual sports but it is not much worth to team sports. I believe there will be – and there is already – a break with the past because Man is a complex being, and when it comes to football, we have to understand that eleven men chasing an objective is completely different from one man doing it. So my methodology was directed towards that purpose. I was influenced in this by my own experiences. Manuel Sérgio, a philosopher and my former teacher in ISEF, was also instrumental in my apprenticeship, because he didn't introduce me to hard paths that I would have to follow or dogmas that I should cling to but to clues to new understandings. But to answer the question directly, after my education I felt the need to choose another path and I chose the path of complexity.

Mourinho's way of being contrasts with a story I read in the book *Natural Born Winners* by Robin Sieger. I believe it's appropriate to tell it here, for a better understanding of what was at stake for Mourinho: passively accept the truths of the "great masters" or, instead, to question and seek his own path.

Everyday before dawn, a wise old monk would go to the temple to pray. Every morning when he started his prayers, the temple cat approached him, rubbed against him and distracted him. One day, the monk decided to take a string and tie the cat to the altar while he was praying. That's exactly what he did, every day, for many years. One day the monk died, but the young monks followed the tradition of tying the cat to the altar every morning during prayers, and when the cat died they got another. After a hundred years tying cats to the altar, someone said: 'This is silly. Why not arrange a statue?'

They got a statue and placed it beneath the altar. One hundred years later, another monk said: 'This statue is so beautiful, so ancient and serving such a wonderful tradition that we should put it on the altar.'

As the years passed, the monks sat and worshipped the cat, even though no one really knew why. The cat had always been there, there should be some reason to worship him. (SIEGER, 2005: 109-10)

We are used to easily accepting what we are told as absolute truths without questioning. The story above is a good example of this. Mourinho's position, when he went to college at 18, is an example of the exact opposite. Maybe it was there that Mourinho started his journey to success.

Mourinho is different, indeed. Nothing is separated, isolated or out of context in his work. Everything is connected. He starts from a systemic basis, finds "the end of the thread" and from there, everything follows in a logical, smooth, almost perfect sequence. This is how Mourinho creates the new way of playing, the new training session, the new man, the new team and the new club. In fact, there are no breaks, interruptions or voids. Let me just give you an example. A player of his team does not cease to be so, just because he is not training or playing. When he is resting, has a day off, is at home or in any social event, he remains a team player, representing the rest of the team and the organization to which he belongs in some way. A professional is always a professional under any circumstances. That intrinsic and constant quality does not take days off or go on holiday just because it's not performing its task in a direct way. In other words, as far as a Mourinho team is concerned, the next match is and must always be there, any time of day or night, as soon as the last match ended. The player is always on the clock, even when he is not playing or training. So, if one of his players is in a nightclub having "a few drinks" on a Wednesday before a match, he's playing that match and he's already playing badly. It is only natural that he will be replaced even before the match starts.

That's why, for Mourinho, his logic of non-separation sees the football season, the league, as a continuum without any kind of intervals. An example of this reasoning is in the letter he always writes to his players at the start of each season:

"It must always be our objective to 'be champions'. It must be a daily objective, a consistent and permanent motivation, and a light that guides our journey from now. Every workout, each match, every minute of our professional and social life must focus on this objective, which I repeat, is OURS."

The story that follows is by Matilde, Mourinho's wife, who helps us understand the manager's commitment to his work, even when he is seemingly taking some downtime.

(...) After the matches in Antas, the two of us usually go out to dinner. At the beginning of dinner he asks me how my day and the kids' day was. In the middle of dinner, he is already talking about football, and by dessert he grabs a piece of paper and starts writing the players and the tactics for the next match. That's just who he is, 'he's hopeless'. He will always be like that...

But the reverse is also true, *i.e.*, work can also be oriented to accommodate the players' personal lives. Here is what Jorge Costa told me, at the time he was still an FC Porto player:

I love my job, but it has a drawback: it prevents me from spending more time with my family. At weekends, when children are more available, I am usually busy with training and matches. Realizing how difficult this was for me, Mourinho, 'managed' yellow cards with me, so that I could miss a match in which I wasn't needed; he also spared me from training for enough days, so that I could take a mini vacation with my family.

Here is a more scientific example, in the broadest sense of the word. Pay attention to the notion of speed and how José Mourinho portrays it, through an example from the perspective of complexity.

We do not consider 'speed' according to the traditional way, i.e., from a purely physiological point of view. We have to consider 'speed' as the analysis or data processing and its execution. Our concern, in terms of 'execution speed', is the contextualized 'speed', in other words, the one that our way of playing requires. This is our great concern. When we are training, we look for real-match situations that bring with them a dominance of this physiological necessity, a necessity for our way of playing. (OLIVEIRA AT AL, 2006:120)

Giving a practical example, Mourinho means:

Who is the fastest man in the world? Let's assume it's Francis Obikwelu, who can run 100 meters in less than 10 seconds. He is very fast and I don't know any football player that could keep up with him in a 100-metre race. However, in a football match, 11 against 11, I think Obikwelu would be the slowest! Here's another example: textbook case of a slow player is Deco[10]. If we were to put him in a 100-metre race with other athletes he would make a fool of himself. He is uncoordinated, has no terminal velocity; muscularly, he's probably loaded with slow twitch muscle fibres instead of fast twitch muscle fibres. However, on the pitch, he is one of the fastest players I know because pure speed has nothing to do with football speed. Speed in football is about analysis of the situation, reaction to stimulus and the ability to identify it. What is stimulus in football? It's the position on the field, the position of the ball, what the opponent will do, the ability to anticipate the action, the awareness of what the opponent will do, the ability to realize which space that opponent will occupy to receive the ball alone, etc. Hence, for example, if one of my players is marking Obikwelu, who has an explosive start compared to football players, that will always force my player to start later when he is unmarked. However, because football is not his area of performance, Obikwelu will, in all likelihood, move to the wrong place; then, my player will be around him when he is able to receive the ball. Analyzing speed this way, a player who is slow from the traditional point of view turns out to be a fast player from a complex perspective because he will run at

---

[10] International player, at this time playing for Chelsea FC. Deco already has victories in the Spanish and Portuguese leagues, as well as having won two European leagues, while at Porto FC and Barcelona FC.

a time when others do not expect, at the right time, at a time that the teammate with the ball needs him to run. All of this is complexity, and Man is a complex whole in his context. Therefore, to me, working on individualized qualities and/or out of context from the complexity of the game is a serious mistake.

That's how things appear to us literally complex. After all, Francis Obikwelu may be a slow athlete. Why? Because a player's speed or slowness is not just a physical issue, you cannot get it only from the neck down. The speed or slowness is something that concerns Man as a complex whole, we have to find it from the top of the head downwards, not from the neck down. Furthermore, it is something intentional, something which is sought, and naturally found. So, in a football game with Mourinho's team, Obikwelu will always be a slow player because his *chip*, his intentionality is not formatted, is not developed to play what a game of football is. On the contrary, his whole – brain and body – is "programmed" to run 100 or 200 meters, not to occupy this or that space in ideal conditions for receiving and passing a football. For this reason, Obikwelu, or any other man, is not the world's fastest man, as journalists and many of us like to say in a Cartesian way. This thing of the fastest in the world does not exist. The question is: fastest in what? Otherwise, we would have to see a skydiver in free fall, before opening the parachute, to find the fastest man in the world. This would be in a Cartesian way, of course.

This is the reason why Mourinho says that, in a reductionist per-spective, by decontextualizing Man from a complex reality, many think they are reducing the complexity of the context and easing the work. For Mourinho, this is the wrong reasoning, since decontextual-ization forgets the basics, which is the game. This matter will become even more perceptible a little further ahead in this chapter, when we explain how Eusébio coached goalkeeper Silvino at Benfica.

The examples mentioned above show a way of being, living and working, and its intrinsic logic and scientific explanation applies glob-ally to all the work Mourinho does. Thus, to speak about his leader-ship is to talk about his work as a whole. It can only be explained if it is contextualized as it is only one more element – very important, even crucial – but only one element of a whole composed by parts. When we try to explain these parts – the leadership, for example – we enter a network that constitutes the entirety of Mourinho's work. Everything is related, interacts, and connects, so everything has to be addressed in greater depth here and there, but everything has to be addressed.

What is the basis of Mourinho's work then?

I argue that, at the level of training and leading football teams, José Mourinho is the first to create a new paradigm of knowledge, the complexity of Edgar Morin, and "carry it" from the field of Philosophy, from the world of ideas, to a concrete human activity.

Accordingly, as a basis to analyse José Mourinho's work – *as per* the perspective of complexity – we start from one of the most powerful concepts that shapes Edgar Morin's vision: "*The whole that is in the part that is in the whole.*" This global and comprehensive vision that tells us we can never understand the parts without understanding the whole and will not understand the whole without simultaneously understanding the parts, must also be regarded through different perspectives: the whole is the result of the interconnection among the parts. The whole is what governs, which shapes the parts. It is the whole, also, that is somehow inscribed and embedded in each part. The isolated parts are worthless; it is the relationship, the connections and interactions between them – not losing sight of the characteristics of each part – that prove decisive in shaping and defining the whole. Finally, the whole is different from the sum of the parts.

It is worth recalling the human genome project and introducing a few questions that may help us clarify the issue of the importance of the parts and their relationship to each other to form the whole.

We observed that we are all 99.9% genetically equal among each other. Our difference gap from a monkey is 2% and only 1% from a mouse. Inevitably the question arises: if only 1% separates us from a mouse, which means we are nearly identical, then what causes the same genes to configure a human in some cases and a mouse in others, when we are two living beings so different from each other? What distinguishes us is not the genes, as proven, but their relationship, their connection, how they interact with each other and with the outside. Likewise we can imagine a shoe factory, for example. In the first month, the production was serialized. The following month, each of the same workers produced the shoes from beginning to end. The parts did not change, just the relation among them. We can easily imagine that everything changed, from the final product to the factory. Nothing was ever the same, the factory ceased to be "that" factory to be a different factory.

Another example, from a different but also adaptable angle, may be the composition of sugar: when the atoms of carbon, oxygen and hydrogen come together they form sugar. A sweet substance emerges from this compound. However, separately, the elements that compose it are not sweet.

From this notion of entirety and deep-networked causality, we can say that everything changes in and with José Mourinho. Who was once, in a Cartesian and therefore reductionist vision, a high competition athlete, ceased to be one with Mourinho. Man as a "complex whole" is constituted in his various facets, in his various characteristics, all of them linked together. With Mourinho, the Cartesian athlete disappears to give place to the physical, psychological, technical, tactical, disciplinary, social, etc., athlete. Whatever the phenomenon one wants to watch, it cannot be seen in isolation, out of context, separately. Remember, the part is worthless. It exists and functions as a member of a group that binds to it, connecting the different parts. Only then, do we have the "whole". By isolating one part, it ceases to have any connection, to make sense and to exist. Life teaches us this principle: we are only alive, we only make sense, and we are only "human" while we have connections with the universe, whichever they might be. When we break them, when our last connection to the whole world around us ends, it is because we are dead and if we die nothing makes sense anymore. An example of this is the content of the letter Mourinho addressed to the players after he arrived at Chelsea in the summer of 2004: "*From now on, every workout, every match, every minute of your social life has to focus on the goal of being champion.*" Mourinho's idea of totality around a purpose is clear. The aim of being champion will always have to be present either at work or in his social life, which concerning Mourinho makes absolutely no difference. The football team itself is not seen in isolation, but rather as an entity, a group with an identity and a project, embedded in a network of relationships and a hierarchy of structures.

The players are not the only ones who win or lose at the end of a match. They would not be there if there were no other structures working at the same time and deeply connected to the same objective. Such structures – the medical department, the football department, the department of observation, the Board, the kitmen, etc. – interact with the team, and the team can only work, in the literal sense of the term, with their cooperation. Hence, his assistant Rui Faria claims that *"only the perfect interaction and the perfect performance of each of these structures allows the final product, which is the match in terms of the team, to work optimally and without hindrance."*

Mourinho does not divide the team between the squad and the reserves, he does not distinguish what is done in the match from what is done during training, he does not clearly separate the communication within the team from the communication with the media. Let us remember the case in the pressroom in the Nou Camp, the capital of Catalonia, when Mourinho's Chelsea played against Barcelona. At the time, by telling reporters beforehand the names of his players as well as his opponent's, Mourinho not only sent the message to his players of his full knowledge of Barcelona, thus motivating and reinforcing confidence in his players, but he also sent his opponent the message *"you have no secrets to me."*

Now, it is not so difficult to understand José Mourinho's philosophy. For him, his player does not play football with the feet only, but largely he plays with the head, so he must understand the game. To understand the game, he must understand life, the world, society, family, religion, politics and so on. Therefore, Mourinho's own words in his biography are understandable when he describes the arrival of his team to Seville to compete in the UEFA Cup final.

> *When we got to the hotel, I noticed that everything was perfect. Antero Henrique and Luís César take their work seriously. The rooms were fantastic, with a motivating decoration and, moreover, about a hundred Scots were staying at our hotel and co-inhabited with us.*

Great! I wanted the players to feel the game from the outset and, since security precluded any exaggerated approach, the presence of opposing fans in our hotel gave us the environment I wanted. It was good for my players to be able to feel the opponent's mood.

(JOSÉ MOURINHO IN LOURENÇO 2004: 170)

History shows that this interaction (Celtic fans / players of FC Porto at the same hotel) for the "Cartesian" manager is impossible. For Mourinho it was not only possible but also desirable, because, in his relationship with the players, Mourinho is not interested in the physical Cartesian athlete but rather the Man athlete "complex whole" in close connection with the reality that surrounds him in its broadest sense – not just within football, but his own life outside football. It is from the individual perception that each person has of their reality that they perceive more and more situations. The way one sees the world influences the way one sees football. Therefore, Mourinho says he wants nothing but intellectually evolved players in his teams. They will only be able to learn and understand the essence of the game through their own culture. Such knowledge cannot be basic in an increasingly complex world.

So, Mourinho assumes a clean break with Cartesian thinking without fear:

I believe there will be, and already is, a break with that past [traditional reductionist perspective applied to football] because Man is a complex being and, when it comes to football, we have to understand that eleven men chasing an objective is completely different from one man chasing an objective.

But if everything is interconnected, interactive, does that mean that Mourinho's coaching is so globalizing that he trains all at the same time, without tactical, technical, physical or mental distinction? Absolutely not. The whole continues to be comprised of parts; it does not annul them, it uses them to the pursuit of its ends. The parts need to be improved, to evolve, to be composed and adjusted, because they are in constant redevelopment.

How did Mourinho solve the problem of training the parts in the whole that is the game he wants to play?

What exists in his work is the concept of "dominant", i.e., the focus on one aspect without forgetting that the "whole" is in action and, therefore, many other properly framed factors are also being worked. Mourinho himself alerted me to this fact: *"When I prepare a training session, I prepare a global activity, always realizing what the implications at the various levels are. So I say that every exercise has a dominant."* This notion of dominant introduced by Mourinho is one of the concepts through which he operationalizes the perspective of complexity in his day-to-day work. In a motivationally dominant training session, Mourinho does not forget other secondary objectives such as tactics. Let us consider an example that he provided in his biography published in 2003, entitled *José Mourinho*. During the 2002/03 season, the match that decided FC Porto's victory in the championship was scheduled for the Stadium of Light, with Benfica. During the preparation for the match Mourinho, FC Porto's manager, surprised his players.

> *To motivate my players, I'm not the kind of coach who opts for 'slogans' like: 'Let's get them, we are the best, etc.' Nothing like that. Regarding the match against Benfica, I delivered a message of complete superiority over our opponent. I knew that whenever Camacho, Benfica's manager, was losing, he would switch Zahovic for Sokota. In my workouts, I prepared my team against Sokota's strikes. Until a surprised player told me: 'But Mister, they don't play with Sokota, they play with Zahovic!!' That was what I wanted to hear, and I immediately replied: 'They play with Zahovic when they are winning. Against us, they will have to play with Sokota, which is Camacho's option when they are losing...'* (MOURINHO IN LOURENÇO 2004: 147-8)

With this example we want to illustrate the scope of Mourinho's work – he aims to train the whole, simultaneously and seamlessly. In the example above, in the pitch, coaching his team, he carried out a clear act of leadership in a motivating way: he knew he was giving a message of confidence in their victory by training in a conditioned but positive manner, since his condition was knowing he would be winning. In that sense, he prepared his players to face Sokota, the one that only played when Benfica was losing. But it was precisely in the motivational/emotional factor that Mourinho's dominant work consisted during the week before the match with Benfica. He did not forget all the others, the ball was there to score goals with, but the prevalence, the dominant here was his players' mental preparation.

We have just illustrated the operationalization of the complexity of Mourinho's work in terms of group interaction. What is true for this subject also applies to another: Man considered individually.

Thus, Mourinho sees the professionals in his team as a complex whole. He does not separate their professional life from their social life:

> *I think that those who feel they need discipline in their team should pursue tactical rigor, the demand for a particular tactical discipline rather then naked and raw disciplinary aspects (punctuality, accuracy, etc.). That's how I get overall discipline.* (OLIVEIRA ET AL 2006:178)

Now we are able to understand the example that opened this chapter. By changing tactical systems, Mourinho sought a disciplinary solution instead of a better tactical one. However, it was through the second solution that he got the first.

Another example has to do with Mourinho's refusal of marking individual opponents, even if they are the best in the world. For a manager that aims to promote solidarity among the players on and off the pitch, he cannot be inconsistent and let a player individually mark an opponent. If that were the case, that player would only worry about his opponent rather than his teammates. The opposite is also true, because the team would no longer worry about this mate as well as the opponent. It would introduce an inadequate component of individualism in the team, hampering the coherence and the group connection, exactly what Mourinho fights against and does not accept (Oliveira *et al* 2006). Read Morin's words that explain José Mourinho's position very well:

The weakening of a global perception leads to the weakening of the sense of responsibility (one tends to be responsible only for his specialized task), as well as a weakening of solidarity (each fails to understand its organic connection) [with the group in which he is inserted] (...).

(MORIN 1999:19)

It is, therefore, through the concept of dominant, that José Mourinho works the whole, his team, nothing separating or dissociating the various aspects of their work, working in a network, in a connection, based on the principle that everything has to do with everything, everything affects everything and everything changes everything. Mourinho sees any phenomenon in its entirety, as a system where there are always subsystems inside subsystems. The club, the team, the player, they all have a global dimension, and that is this entirety operationalized by applying the perspective of complexity to his work. Mourinho sees the trees-and-the-forest at the same time as the forest-and-the-trees, which is the same as saying that Mourinho sees the club-and-team-and-the-players while he sees the players-and-team-and-club. This vision is reflected in Morin's language by the sentence *"the whole that is the part that is whole."*

Thus, one realizes the extent that the football player acquires for Mourinho. For him, the player, the athlete has a global dimension, he is a system or a subsystem of other subsystems, or systems, depending on the universe where we put him. In any case, there is always an overall dimension.

It's in this whole, which is the outcome of applying the perspective of complexity to his work, that Mourinho uses his players' actions. His player must reflect socially what he is professionally, and the opposite is also true. He will only be disciplined on the pitch, inserted in his group, if he behaves the same way off the pitch and vice-versa. It is in this global context that we understand the complex individual that is the human being. For Mourinho, the player is a whole, part of another whole, which is the team, with physical, technical and psychological characteristics to be developed as a whole. This is how the manager does not separate the physical from the psychological, so he does not work either aspect separately or in an out of context way. Moreover, nothing is separated or out of context in his work. Let us consider an example given by Mourinho himself:

Some people still think that by reducing the complexity, things become easier. I think we are only creating the conditions for the player's success during training, which is not transferred to the pitch. For example, 15 years ago Eusébio was coaching Silvino, Benfica's goalkeeper. Eusébio placed the ball near the penalty area and shot at goal to train the goalkeeper. The problem was that Silvino could not train because all the balls went in. He simply couldn't train because the attempts were out of context from what the game naturally is; a player does not stand 100 times isolated against the goalkeeper to provide optimal shot. This situation is out of context with the reality and the complexity of the game. However, there are many coaches who do this as a training session. I completely disagree, because the situation is fictional, and out of context with the reality of the game, where players always have to be aware of the opponent. So I never do things like that. I have to create the conditions for integrated training where I am working the complexity of the game through situations as close to reality as possible, i.e. of what is expected to happen in the game. So when I work on my players' shooting, I put the opponents right there, because that's what happens in the game. Before shooting, my player has the opponent ahead and has to overcome him and only then can he make the shot. This way I'm turning the exercise into a match itself. Not only am I working on shooting and training my forwards, but also my midfielders, my goalkeeper and my defenders who will have to face strikers in matches. So I do not put my goalkeeping coach shooting alone at goal to train my goalkeeper, because this situation is repetitive stimuli and the match has none of this.

Eusébio's shots were out of context from what the game is, as "*a player does not stand a hundred times isolated against the goalkeeper to provide optimal shots*". This training situation is out of context from the reality and the complexity of the game. For Mourinho, this is a fictitious situation because players have to pay attention to their opponents in the match. Mourinho tries to create conditions for integrated training, where he can work on the complexity of the game through situations as close as possible to the reality, i.e. as close as possible to "what one hopes the match will be" (Mourinho). With a different approach, another example of non-separation of the physical from the psychological is given to us by Mourinho in response to a journalist from *O Jogo*, when he asked him whether his team – FC Porto – was in decent physical shape. Mourinho said: *"I can't talk about that. I don't know where the physical ends and the psychological or the tactical begins. For me, football is a whole just like Man."* (Mourinho *in* Oliveira *et al* 2006: 40).

The traditional factors that are trainable come up in the whole that is the training, embedded in a work that has directly to do with the game you want to play. We can understand when Mourinho talks about the sprinter Francis Obikwelu being a slow player on a football pitch. His muscle mass, speed and explosion can never overcome the speed of thought, the position on the pitch and the ability to anticipate moves typical of a football player, simply because his whole is not ready for that, is not contextualized in that kind of mental, physical, psychological, emotional, global effort etc., that football requires and is.

By expanding the analysis that we have been doing out of the whole that the football player is for the whole that the group is, Mourinho's logic remains unchanged. Here too, the part – the player – can only be seen and contextualized in / for the group. The group is the most important thing, and the part matters while serving the whole. Here, the global assumes the collective term, so the part can and must be sacrificed in favour of the whole since the evolution of the part is not conceivable without being at the same level and stage of evolution of the whole. However, the whole must also be the context that offers each player, each part, the manifestation of his uniqueness. Therefore, the individual is also very important. It is not about not seeing the wood (the team) by only seeing the trees (the players), it's about seeing the-trees-and-the-wood.

Indeed, a lot could be said about complexity here. Edgar Morin, devoted a lifetime to this subject and a thousand pages would not be enough to cover it. However, Complexity is not our concern. What is important here is Mourinho's leadership and complexity is the tool that helps us to understand his work. So, without deep explanations, what we need is the key to understand this leadership. In order to understand Mourinho's relationship with the typology of his groups, we need to retain the idea of the whole – a whole that controls the parts and is different from their sum.

This strong idea of the whole governing the parts is crucial in understanding how Mourinho works in the group towards another whole that is the match. In this sense, Training is not viewed merely as preparation for the match, but as a part of the whole, which is the process of playing, of training and then of playing. Here, Mourinho introduces us to the idea of training as projection / representation of a real match. For example, the training lasts as long as a match, his assistant Rui Faria told me: "*We seek maximum performance and concentration for an hour and a half of training – the exact duration of a match – thereby keeping the player concentrated for 90 minutes.*" The complexity of the processes that Rui Faria's notion involves: the idea of a training session that lasts as long as a match is an adaptation of mental effort, rather than physical effort, or better still, of overall human effort. The dominant focus is concentration. Physical fitness will eventually occur naturally, framed in a wider mental, psychological and emotional phenomenon. In that broader phenomenon, which makes the projection of the training/anticipation of the match, we include the issue of unpredictability, that Mourinho wants to reduce as much as possible. Only a training session, as a perspective of a match, can bring up situations that are unpredictable, impossible or difficult to plan for, and that, once trained, can be transferred to the match, thereby working on this same unpredictability. If training is like the match, the unforeseen aspects of the match are also the unforeseen aspects of training. Therefore, when the match is being played through this "representation" of reality, whatever was unpredictable during training, ceases to be unpredictable during the match itself. We are not talking about reaching a situation of no unpredictability. The intention here is to minimize, as far as possible, unforeseen circumstances that may arise, because for Mourinho what is most difficult in the match is to be confronted with unknown situations. In short, as Mourinho stated: "*because the unknown is always uncomfortable, unpredictability [the unknown] relates to what you do and what you're prepared to do, and what others do and what you presume they can do."*

The aim is to try to practice before – in training – what you think will happen next – in the match. Take note, training regarded globally as Mourinho sees it, *is* like the match. Moreover, training *is the* match, intensely... So, Mourinho does not do practice matches in his training sessions, meaning a normal match of 11 against 11, like in a football match. The training is sectoral, *i.e.,* focused on the situation(s) that Mourinho wants to train. What happens at a given time during a football match is a specific situation, not the entire game at the same time. Either they are in midfield, in transition with other teams trying to gain control of the ball, or a team attacks and the other defends, or there is a counter-attack, etc. These are real situations, dominant situations, that Mourinho trains, emphasizing a particular aspect in every training session. For example, if the dominant is defence, Mourinho chooses the sector pitch where the defence is, and projects the game situation on that zone with strikers, midfielders and the goalkeeper. Thus, he trains the defence and also the rest of the sectors of the game in the context of this particular situation. This approach has several advantages over the match itself. In addition to maintaining a global approach to the game, the game simulation gets more intense. By dwindling the pitch and focusing on just a given situation, it makes the players share the ball more often than in the real situation. From this situation, there is also an increase of unforeseen situations, which will reduce the unpredictability of the match itself. Therefore, training is not only *the* match, it is also an intense match. *"The player can only play on the edge if he trains on the edge... and the match reflects the training session. The greater the determination is in the training, the greater it is in the game"*, Rui Faria told us. Again, in the context of high complexity, Mourinho's whole idea applies here: by playing through the training session, they play the match in the same way. A player can become a great football player by playing football a lot, and doing it well. In Mourinho's words, this is a clear idea. In Israel, when Shimon Peres invited him, he told the audience: *"A great pianist doesn't run around the piano nor does push-ups with his fingertips. He plays the piano to be great. He plays his entire life. Being a great player doesn't mean running, doing sit-ups or other exercises. The best way to be a great player is to play football."*

3. LEADERSHIP THEORIES APPLIED TO MOURINHO'S WORK

I have always seen him as a great manager and, more than that, a great leader.

(PINTO DA COSTA, FC PORTO'S CHAIRMAN IN LOURENÇO, 2003:98)

LEADERSHIP TODAY

Leadership is trendy. It is an ever-present subject. Have you noticed that for a few years now there hasn't been a day when you have not spoken of, heard of or read the words leader or leadership? You may not have realized it, but when you read the morning paper, when you see the news on TV, or even when you mention any political, sports or even social subjects with a friend or co-worker, you read, say or hear the word leader or leadership. Is that strange? Maybe not.

The concept of leadership has come in our lives relatively recently, and its linguistic profusion – at least in Portugal and in the more developed countries – has been evident. In fact, I think the word has even been trivialized, so it is doubtful that it is always used correctly, or in its proper context. Even the concept raises questions, for its numerous, often discrepant, theoretical approaches. No wonder there is difficulty in defining, or even drawing a profile of leadership. Let us do a little exercise, then:

Which criteria really matter? Let's say it's time to elect a new world leader. Here are some facts about the three leading candidates:

Candidate A associates with crooked politicians and consults with astrologers. He's had two mistresses. He chain-smokes and drinks eight to 10 martinis a day.

Candidate B was kicked out of the college twice, used opium as an undergraduate, now sleeps until noon, and drinks a quart of whiskey every evening.

Candidate C is a decorated war hero. He's a vegetarian, doesn't smoke, drinks only an occasional beer, and hasn't had any extra-matrimonial affairs.

Whom did you chose? If you opted for **C**, *you may be surprised at what you get:*

Candidate A is Franklin D. Roosevelt
Candidate B is Winston Churchill
Candidate C is Adolf Hitler" (KETS DE VRIES 2001: 280)

This is a small, simple exercise, but it reminds and alerts us to the fact that, throughout history, many mistakes were made when choosing leaders. However, because we live in a world that is changing, we have an increasing need for leaders, whether they are politically, culturally, economically or socially motivated. The change is here to stay. Things have changed so much in recent decades; our lives have been turned upside down. I'll give you two examples: 60 years ago my grandparents' generation travelled in the interior of Portugal, in carts pulled by oxen. My parents' generation put a man on the moon. My generation has reached Mars... Another example, equally or even more shocking: today, we are more exposed to a ton of information when we open any national daily newspaper, than any human being from the Middle Ages would be throughout his life. At that time, a man or woman couldn't access the volume of information that the "Diário de Notícias" contains within its pages.

Without any doubt change has arrived, settled in and did not ask for permission. Change is not a new phenomenon but, nowadays, it takes place at an exponentially higher speed, giving a larger and clearer perception of the phenomenon. However, change is the unknown, the path that takes us out of our comfort zone to places we do not know about, and that make us uncomfortable. Our first reaction to change is anxiety; therefore, our first reflex is to look for someone who can guide us to contain that anxiety. Thus, when change and anxiety invade our world, the conditions for the emergence of leadership are created (Kets de Vries 2001).

We need leaders in virtually all aspects of our lives. Sport is no exception, quite the contrary. The theories that explain this are many and varied, from sport as an escape to sport as a kind of substitute for war or even a new form of warfare. In a way or another, sport also generates leaders who are worshiped and followed all over the world. José Mourinho, the case study of this book, fits perfectly in this notion of leader. A man both loved and hated, adored or criticized almost everywhere in the world; for better or for worse, he leaves no one indifferent, and therefore influences millions of humans directly or indirectly.

From the perspective of complexity, Mourinho's leadership can and should be understood through its various and multiple relationships with other aspects of his work. Using Mourinho's own terminology, in this chapter we will see leadership as a *dominant*, which stands in a *whole* without decontextualizing it, so you never lose sight of the overall work of the manager.

Worldwide, Mourinho's leadership has been one of the most discussed aspects of his work. The consensus is almost unanimous: Mourinho is a great leader. There have been many diverse, and sometimes contradictory, explanations for this fact. Apart from the book *Mourinho: Porquê Tantas Vitórias?* (Oliveira et al 2006), which relates – albeit superficially (because that wasn't its purpose, so this is not a criticism of the authors' work, quite the contrary) – Mourinho's leadership to the paradigm of complexity, no other work on the subject could touch on the subject that I developed in my Masters Degree's thesis (2007) and I still do: the practice and study of Mourinho's leadership from the perspective of complexity. For me, the common analyses of José Mourinho's leadership are wrong. They separate what cannot be separated, based on a reductionist view and analysing the subject in a traditional way, by isolating its various aspects, separating them from a whole that cannot be separated or divided. To help me in this chapter, to better understand the integrated leadership of Mourinho, I asked for some friends' help – former football players, who have two factors in common: they were led by Mourinho and are in leadership positions today. I'm referring to Vítor Baía, FC Porto's current director of external relations with a Bachelors Degree in Sports Leadership and Jorge Costa, who followed a career as a Football Manager. I also asked for the help of two other major players. I'm referring to the former Portuguese international Deco and Didier Drogba, the Ivory Coast international. I talked to them in London and they helped me understand Mourinho, because both their lives have been strongly influenced by him. Finally, of course, José Mourinho's help with another unpublished interview on the subject of leadership, "his" leadership. Everyone helped me – and will help the reader – with their unique and pragmatic perspective, to better understand José Mourinho's leadership.

THE MEANING OF LEADERSHIP

A boss creates fear, a leader confidence. A boss fixes blame, a leader corrects mistakes. A boss knows all, a leader asks questions. A boss makes work drudgery, a leader makes it interesting. A boss is interested in himself or herself, a leader is interested in the group. (RUSSEL H. EWING, ENGLISH JOURNALIST, 1885-1976)

The word leader is associated with power and, according to its etymology, means the one who shows the way. It's a formal power – the power to give orders, to decide, to demand, etc., – but it's also an informal power, which translates into the natural ability that someone has to influence others. Mourinho's leadership is mainly based on this second form of power. In fact, I really think his informal power is the basis of all his formal power. To better understand the issue and Mourinho, I'll talk about a new concept I have been writing about, and I drew from Joseph S. Nye Jr., in his book *Liderança e Poder*, where the author establishes the difference between *Soft Power and Hard Power*.

The latter is defined as a power that "is based on incentives (rewards) and threats" while the first is characterized by "achieving the desired results captivating others rather than manipulating or threatening them."

It seems obvious that this concept is the largest part of Mourinho's power characteristics. Quoting Jorge Costa, after having asked him about the truly special relationship José Mourinho always keeps with his players: *"How does this happen? I do not know... you feel it. It's almost like when someone falls in love, and love is hard to explain, isn't it? These are such pure, such natural relationships, that the explanation becomes complicated."* This is why Nye Jr. says *"leadership is not simply a matter of issuing orders, but it also involves guidance by example and attracting others to fulfil a particular role"*. In truth, if leading were a question of ordering, everything would be easy. Anyone with power to issue orders would be a leader. That is not how it works. Mourinho himself said:

What is leadership? To me, leadership is not to give orders, it is to lead, to guide. I'll compare it with parenthood to explain myself better. You can be a father by ordering or by guiding. Any parent now tries to make their child learn by himself, find the way without having to issue orders. It's castrating to issue orders. I'm going to play treasure hunt with my son. I won't tell him where the treasure is, otherwise the game will lose all its leisure and educational value. He must strive to find the treasure. He must do what's in his power to be able to gather the necessary clues. When he found it, through the clues I provided him, he was happy because he had discovered it, rather than me telling him where it was. If I had told him where the treasure was in the beginning, I would've castrated a range of skills from him that sooner or later, would make him discover the treasure and take another step in his development as a human being.

Applying this concept to my work, I don't want to castrate them, quite the contrary; I want to develop skills both at individual and collective level. So I don't issue orders, I guide. In my view, guiding is a route that gives some flexibility on both behavioural and mental levels. Therefore, the players don't feel handcuffed, they enjoy some freedom. If they are shackled, they can't move and they're dominated by someone. The day that someone – if that happens – takes the shackles, they'll be lost and won't know what to do. What I want is to prepare them for the autonomy they'll need to have in their life and on the pitch. They have 90 minutes of autonomy per week, and my action during those 90 minutes is extremely limited. At that time they must have power of decision and decide. They must have creative skills and create. None of this is achieved with shackles, so I guide them, allowing them to develop their skills at an individual and collective level.

In the same line of thinking – as reinforcement of the central idea of trying to approach the concepts of leadership and power – the world famous scientist and author, Fritjof Capra says that the task of leadership is to facilitate the process of emergency and, in doing so, to promote creativity: *"This means creating conditions rather than giving orders, and using the power of authority to empower others."*

In short, these two authors as well as José Mourinho present us with concepts which, properly framed, convey the same idea: that effective leadership facilitates and fosters individual consciousness – the basis of creativity!

SPECIAL ONE – A GLOBAL CONCEPT

To be great, be whole: nothing that is you
Should you exaggerate or exclude.
In each thing, be all. Give all you are
In the least you ever do.
The whole moon, because it rides so high,
Is reflected in each pool.

(FERNANDO PESSOA – RICARDO REIS POETRY, 14.2.1933)

José Mourinho is the "Special One". This concept, as indeed many others at this level, attempts to capture the leader in its entirety, in all its aspects. José Mourinho is the "Special One", a notion that is not translated into anything definite but, in qualitative terms, marks his way of being. The "Special One" is the way people look at him as a whole, one that goes beyond the restricted line of the football coach. We believe that this is how José Mourinho is seen by most people, although possibly in a more intuitive and instinctive manner, rather than analytically or reflected. When people criticize him, when they support him, when they talk about him, people do not talk about the coach, the communicator or the leader only. They talk about José Mourinho, a whole, for better or worse, they talk about the "Special One", a whole that makes him what he is as a human being and as a manager. As Professor Manuel Sérgio rightly intuits in a happily rich compilation of texts – *Textos Insólitos* – "*the way the man is triumphs in the coach he can be*". Precisely for this reason, the "Special One" is not the coach but the global and complex man that has already succeeded as a coach, with all the victories and trophies he has already won. However, the "Special One", this global notion of the man José Mourinho is, did not only triumph as a manager; he triumphed as a father, husband, son, friend and leader as well.

If the leader triumphed – we are now moving towards the eye of the storm, the essence of Mourinho's leadership – he would never have been able to do it alone. And it's not only him! As John U. Bacon wrote in his fantastic book *Cirque du Soleil – The Spark – Igniting the Creative Fire* That Lives Within Us All (p.121):

> *A trapeze artist could never lift without the specialized work of her riggers and coaches. A contortionist could never make the audience embark on a journey of imagination if not for her makeup artists and the wardrobe that mingled her character and her representation in such a colourful union. Every scene, every movement, every moment was the culmination of the efforts of hundreds of people.*

Nowadays there are no one-person victories, even in individual sports. Whatever the sport or business area, the victories and defeats are always, directly or indirectly, the responsibility of a team that works towards achieving the common goal. In my opinion, that is why leadership is, in essence, a complex social process (composed of various systems), systemic (systems that relate to each other continuously, always evolving) and contextual (the actions of the leader depend and adapt to the context; so, a single leader can act differently in similar situations if inserted in a different context. Example: a dismissal in China is not the same as a dismissal in Western Europe). As a complex social process, it involves leaders and followers, ordinary men and women in situations more or less common or unusual. Therefore, we begin to understand why nothing can be out of context, nor separate, and why everything is articulated and interactive. We begin to understand the importance of the whole in Mourinho, and it is easy to frame, at least theoretically, the perspective of complexity.

THE LEADER IS HUMAN

Leading comes in many ways. People like Franklin Roosevelt sweep us away with their speeches. Others, like Joe Di Maggio, lead by example. Both Winston Churchill and Douglas MacArthur were exceptionally brave and excellent speakers. Ronald Reagan's leadership involved strength and consistency of his character, and people followed him because they believed in him. Ultimately, we will eventually find out which techniques and approaches work better, and this teaching will come from those whom we intend to lead. A good part of our ability to get people to do what they should depends on what they see when they look at us. We need to see someone who is stronger, but also human. (GIULIANI, 2003:13-4).

In the first months after his arrival in London to manage Chelsea, José Mourinho did not feel comfortable with the fact that driving is on the left in England. When he needed to move around in the city, he took a taxi. One day, Mourinho entered a London taxi and a few minutes later the somewhat incredulous taxi driver said: *"You're just like José Mourinho, don't know if you know him, he's Chelsea's manager."* José Mourinho remained silent, while he watched the man staring at him, suspiciously. They were both silent for a few seconds. Then, as though he had suddenly found the answer, the driver stared at Mourinho again, squinted his right eye and exclaimed triumphantly: *"Hummm, impossible, it can't be Mourinho. People like him don't take cabs! ..."*

Since leadership is a social process, the leader must necessarily be human like everyone else, with his life cycle longer or shorter, his flaws and virtues, his health, his illnesses, his charisma or lack of it, etc. Obviously, he has different personality traits, but is it not exactly like that with all of us, leaders or not? His unique characteristics make him different in what distinguishes us from each other: the fact that each and every one of us is special and unique. Clearly, leadership (continuous leadership) takes place among and with people. Leadership is not something that someone – the leader –might possess, or that many – followers – can also make. Leadership is something that belongs to all of those involved in a particular process, in a particular place and time (social process). In this process each person plays his or her role, and the leader is undoubtedly the main actor because he is the facilitator of collective purpose. For better or for worse, all the attention and all the limelight are focused on him. However, one danger is the temptation of "deification." The leader is an increasingly newsworthy human being. That is easy to understand. That's how journalism gets an important income. The leader is becoming increasingly, and with better results, a product to be sold. The leader, the true and authentic leader, must learn to resist the natural drift and narcissistic exhibitionism and know exactly and in every moment what his place in this world is.

On August 20, 2009, Jamaican Usain Bolt broke the world record in the 200 meters at the World Championships in Athletics, in Berlin, Germany. This record came just days after the same Usain Bolt broke (in the same competition), the world record of 100 meters.

When he won the 200-meter sprint, it was clear that Usain Bolt was the hero of Berlin's World Championships. Minutes after winning the medal and the world record, a journalist, – maker of such idols and myths that sell millions of newspapers – asked him, before millions of viewers around the world: *"Do you feel like a superman?"* With a slight smile on his still sweaty face and genuine humility, Bolt replied: *"No, I don't feel like a superman. I just feel like a man who runs fast..."*

Besides showing that true leadership is human, this reply illustrates a way of being, a way to see oneself and relate to others, to be a leader and, in particular, it is an excellent influence to the listener. And it teaches us another principle, one that we can go unnoticed, but that is as real as it is important: today, no one is the best anymore.

It is the relationship with people that makes Mourinho – and obviously Usain Bolt and many others – special. It is the way he attracts, communicates, and connects with his tribe. A connection that is well defined in Vítor Baía's words, when I asked him about Mourinho's relationship with his players:

> *We have always looked at him as a common man. Moreover, he himself has never cultivated this way of being and we were well aware who the leader was, but we also knew that we could laugh and play when it was time for that. This was, after all, one of his characteristics, even on a personal level. He liked fun and games a lot. He teased everyone in a playful way. Many times, he teased deputies with big pranks. And we made the best of this and spent quite a few fun moments, even at work.*
> Then, you saw him as a normal human being, like any other...
> *Of course...*

Jorge Costa says the same thing. Mourinho is a normal man, but normal in a different way, that's why he's a leader:

> *We have always seen him as a regular guy, not a superman. However, we also looked up to him with great admiration. We accepted him unconditionally as our leader. We felt that there was something different about him, and admired him. I don't know if it's what he said, the image that he showed, maybe both, but mainly because of a very important asset he has: his decisions, his decision-making capacity, when everything felt right... For me, Mourinho is someone whom I look up to, and, even him not being one of my best friends, he's someone I see as a friend and, professionally, as someone different, and this difference is characterized by a number of factors.*

... Jorge Costa continues, still about the connections Mourinho establishes with his group:

He acts in a perfectly natural way with the players. I remember what happened with me when we played the final of the Champions League and scored the 3-0. I went to the bench and hugged Mourinho. This is what it is difficult to understand. In football, we talk about 'ass-kissing' a lot, but my gesture had nothing to do with that and it's even difficult to understand that scenario: in the Champions League final, after the team scored the third goal, why would the team captain hug the manager instead of his teammates, and tell him a sponta-neous and heartfelt manner: 'You deserve it, you're the greatest!'? To me, he was and will always be the greatest. How does this happen? I don't know... you feel it. It's almost like when someone falls in love, and love is hard to explain, isn't it? These are such pure, such natural relationships, that the explanation becomes complicated.

Portuguese international Deco, Brazilian born, also talks about the special relationship Mourinho has with the players. Trained by José Mourinho in FC Porto, Deco recalls Mourinho's deep knowledge of his team and the control he got from that knowledge.

What struck me the most was the psychological control he had over all the players. He knew exactly how he had to act with each of the players. He knew that sometimes he had to be tough with one player or another, and he had the perfect notion of how that would reflect on the game itself. He also knew how he could 'empower' a player, to dis-cuss the tactics of the game without losing authority, raising the morale of the player in question because he knew that, due to his personality traits, that player needed that kind of stimulus. What I thought was fantastic was that control, that perception he had, of how far he could push any player and therefore achieve his maximum efficiency. And I'm not talking in technical or tactical terms, but rather in psycholog-ical terms. In that aspect, he knew exactly how to bring the best out of everyone.

In the end, the effective leader is the one that brings out the best everyone has within oneself, who makes each one prove oneself and give one's best for the group, for the objectives of the organization.

That is why it has been said and written that Mourinho has the ability to transform average teams into super teams and average players into super players. For this to happen – and we speak of a social process among ordinary people – the leader must be connected to the people around him. This connection begins with the emergence of leadership and evolves as the contexts allow it. I personally believe that Mourinho's leadership emerged in FC Porto, as I mentioned before.

I remember José Mourinho's arrival at FC Porto. The club was far from its glory days, and the president Jorge Nuno Pinto da Costa, tried to return to their winning ways. Pinto da Costa decided to fire manager Octávio Machado, who had got only an exasperating 6th place at the start of the second round of the championship. Furthermore, the club had not been champion for three consecutive years. Such poor performance had only been seen in the late 70s. For the first time in about 20 years as the president, Pinto da Costa also began to be challenged by the supporters. He then supported José Mourinho, certain that that season was compromised, but hoping better times would come. The sports weakness the club was going through did not frighten José Mourinho. On January 23, 2002, the day of his presentation to members and journalists, José Mourinho risked everything and said: "*I'm sure next year we'll be champions.*"

And the following year FC Porto won the National Championship, the Portuguese Cup and the UEFA Cup (the first time a Portuguese club had won this competition). Mourinho promised less than what he accomplished.

For me, that moment and those words were the emergence of José Mourinho's leadership – as it still emerges today.

The club was starved for victories and needed a change. By promising victory, Mourinho anticipated the future, and assumed a vision, a winning project, ambitious and tangible, because what matters is not the greatness of the goal or dream, but how realistic it is and that everyone can believe in its realization. Mourinho did nothing more than promise a shiny future for FC Porto. And, in doing so, he took a risk and was heavily criticised by his opponents. However, to his tribe, to his players and to the fans, the message of hope and ambition was clear. Everyone believed him, and everyone followed him after that. A leadership emerged then, so strong that even when he made a mistake – because to err is human, and when we talk about leaders we are talking about human beings – these errors missed sensitive personal damage.

Therefore, it was through the promise – with apparent personal risk – of a better, more attractive and promising future, that the new FC Porto coach began his connection with fans, directors, players and staff of FC Porto. In doing so, he saw and felt the emergence of his leadership, his way of being in the club at that moment. It was the beginning of that social process, a process that involved many ordinary people, from top to bottom, that gave such good results: the best ever in two years, in the history of the club. Moreover, Mourinho's story as a FC Porto leader is made of connections, of interactivity and exchanges between him and his followers. That story turned everyone's strengths into one single strength: everyone's weaknesses into everyone's strengths; everyone's weaknesses into the everyone's strengths. This was only possible thanks to this permanent and continuous connection in a group that is built as a system.

One can see how José Mourinho has always joined the clubs, in his press conference presentation, wherever he went. Let us consider the last three (FC Porto, Chelsea FC and Inter Milan FC) and see how his mark was soon mercilessly stamped as his initial attitude sealed the relationship he would have, not only with the club, the players and the fans, but also with the countries of those clubs.

His sentence at FC Porto *"I'm sure next year we'll be champions"*; his statement at Chelsea "I am a Special One"; his first press conference at Inter, given in an irreproachable Italian. Three cultures, three contexts, and three attitudes that dictated and conditioned, from the outset, Mourinho's future and that of all his followers. The truth is that these three clubs were champions immediately after. As for reactions to these three moments, they are illustrative of how Mourinho has left its mark and immediately connected with his followers. About his arrival at FC Porto, Deco, a player at that time, would later write in his biography:

José Mourinho's arrival at FC Porto allowed me to see something I had never seen before: at no point in my career, had I seen players so happy with the arrival of a new coach. Even more so, because José Mourinho infected everyone with his way of being, of living, and of working. His methods were appealing, the training sessions were exciting, and early on, we felt that, with him, things were going to work. (...) Early on, we also felt that José Mourinho's famous statement on the day of his presentation had not been made in vain. For those who don't remember, here it is: "Next year, we'll be champions!" Some people called him arrogant, but, early on, I felt that it was a manifestation of self-confidence. Time would eventually prove him right...

(ALVES, 2003: 125, 125)

His arrival at Chelsea was also discussed by vice-captain Frank Lampard in his autobiography entitled *Totally FRANK*. Symptomatic of what I've been defending here, is that Frank Lampard devoted an entire chapter to José Mourinho, whom he decided to call: "The Special One". What Lampard wrote about the "Special One" is also revealing. The English player was in the preparation stage of the England squad for Euro 2004:

I saw his introduction as Chelsea manager on television the same as everyone else. Myself, JT [John Terry], Bridgey [Wayne Bridge] and Joe Cole[119] were holed up in the England team hotel in Manchester preparing for Euro 2004 when Mourinho exploded in our lives. I watched his performance in the press conference at Stamford Bridge and thought he came across as arrogant and very confident but I don't have a problem with that when someone has the medals in their locker to back it up. (...) From the moment I saw him handle the media on his first day at Chelsea I knew that there was something which set him apart from everyone else. (LAMPARD, 2006: 309, 313)

---

[11] John Terry, Wayne Bridge and Joe Cole along with Lampard were 4 Chelsea players who were part of the England team managed by Swede Sven-Goran Eriksson.

Finally, his arrival in Italy. The posture, the message, but above all, speaking fluent Italian. This first contact resulted in the text of the famous *La Gazzetta dello Sport*, written by journalist Riccardo Pratesi. The title tells us a lot already: "E' SUBITO MOURINHO-SHOW "NÉ SPECIALE, NÉ PIRLA". After the beginning, the heading was highlighted:

Prima spettacolare conferenza stampa, in italiano, del nuovo tecnico dell'Inter: 'Sono Mourinho e basta. Sono arrivato in un clube speciale (...) .' Brillante, sicuro di sè, padrone di un italiano già eccelente. Josè Mourinho non si smentisce. Si presenta alla stampa con una conferenza fiume di 45'.

Regarding connections and contexts, I also remember the defeat at home against Panathinaikos.

In 2003, with FC Porto, his team lost at home in the quarter-finals of the UEFA Cup, 0-1, with Panathinaikos. At the end of the match, Mourinho saw Sergio Markarian, the opposing coach, celebrating as if he had won the tie. He did not like what he saw, and immediately went over to his opponent:

'Don't celebrate too soon, this isn't over.' Shortly afterwards, he passed by Porto fans in Estádio das Antas, and signalled to them, as if to say 'take it easy, we're not done...' (...) When he arrived at the dressing room after seeing the Greek celebrations, he was faced with the opposite. His players were sad, frustrated and their heads were down. José Mourinho wanted to make things very clear there and then. 'This isn't over. I just told their coach that. We'll turn this around, and if anyone here doesn't believe that it is possible to win there and move on to the semi-finals, tell me now, because you'll stay here and I'll go to Greece with some one else.' (LOURENÇO 2004: 151)

In the days that followed, as Mourinho reported, *"people charged me [the victory in Greece after what I had told them] until our match in Greece. They would meet me on the street and say:* 'Mister, do not forget who said it is not finished yet. We have to go there to win, we believe...'"

Fifteen days later, FC Porto won the match 2-0, qualifying for the UEFA Cup semi-finals. They would go on to win that year's competition.

Six years later, when I interviewed Vítor Baía, that was one of the examples he gave me to illustrate the ability to motivate, to influence and how Mourinho's relationship with his followers is deeply striking:

> *I remember when the match with Panathinaikos ended at Antas's stadium, and we lost 0-1. We saw him leave his seat to go and greet their coach, and we didn't know what he might say. Later, he arrived at the dressing room and told us. He used it to motivate us, because we were dead by that point. Losing that match at home was a tremendous blow, devastating us. However, we were aware that he said something to the Greeks' coach, and also made some signs for our fans, came to the dressing room and told us everything, before he assured us that the second round would have to be won: 'I have warned their coach', i.e., he wasn't greeting him, he told him we were not done and that we were going to Greece to win. I also recall that he walked by Chainho[12][10] and told him: 'Warn your teammates that are all celebrating, that this 'shit' is not over yet. We'll go there and we'll win!' He arrived at the dressing room and the first thing he told me was: 'Chin up, we'll go there to win', and then he remarked, 'I have already warned their coach, and their players that we'll go there to win, and I turned to our fans and said the same thing.'*
>
> *We were dead by this point, and that was something that raised our morale in an absolutely amazing way. To the point that, when I got home my wife and some friends were there, all with very low morale, and my immediate reaction was to ask them: 'Do you want to bet that we'll go there to win?'*

---

[12] Chainho was a Portuguese player, formerly of FC Porto, and was playing for Panathinaikos at that time.

We could mention many other examples here, but these are suf-ficient to demonstrate the connection and relationship (dependent and interdependent) that Mourinho, as a leader, has with his follow-ers, both who work with him directly and whom he influences indi-rectly. The leader's connection with his followers is, in my view, the utterly decisive factor nowadays; it is essential for effective leadership. Mourinho masters this part. Why? For all that has been said and much more, but if there is something that defines him as a leader, something that affects everything is that Mourinho is a leader in the centre of the circle and not at the top of the pyramid. This notion of leader-ship position, that conditions everything, rests upon the idea that today's leaders are not on top of a pyramid, but rather, in the centre of the circle – something which I have been advocating. In other words, the effective leader is, organically and psychologically, in the middle of a complex web of relationships. One of the topics I discussed with Didier Drogba was this positioning and also Mourinho's relation-ship with his players. Pay attention to the comparison that Drogba draws here:

He is very close to the players and this is why they will reciprocate. He is different from other managers who always have a straight face. He laughs with the players, tells jokes; those of us who work with him on a daily basis, see him in a way that people outside can't see.

How was his relationship with you guys, emotionally? People say he is very emotional...

Yes, he's a very emotional man. It was almost common to see him celebrating a goal like a player. That's why he was able to understand what the players did. For example, in France, before a match, a player had a problem with his daughter and he said 'ok, go home, see your daughter, get your problem solved, and come back when everything is settled. These are small details, but they mean a lot to a player and make him the coach he is.

These small details remind you of your first meeting with Mourinho.

Yes, we were in a small room, we talked about many things and in the end he told me something I'll never forget: "You are a good striker, but if you want to be one of the world's best, for you to be on top, you have to come to Chelsea to work with me."

And he keeps his promises. Keeping promises is very important. Indeed, you are one of the best strikers in the world now.

Thank you (chuckles). Yes, keeping promises is critical, especially if we say to a player he will be what he really wants to be. That's why I'll be eternally grateful to him. Those weren't empty words. He saw qualities in me that, indeed, could make me achieve the level where I am today. He saw my potential, still unrealized, but which would make me what I am today. No doubt, he saw it and helped me to develop my potential.

Deco also speaks of personal needs within a group and Mourinho's permanent attention to them.

He doesn't ask how to train. He adapts to the players' physical and mental fatigue. Often, he gives us time off because he sees that we need it. Once, he told me 'go to Brazil for 3 or 4 days'. It's like I say, this is a very deep knowledge of how each player reacts, and of what he needs. In my case, I returned as pleased as punch, needing to repay what he had done for me. So he has this perception of everything and this also happens during training. He asks how the players are, how they feel here or there on the pitch...

But does he involve the players in the project that is the team?

Yes, because he imagines a day when you'll be tired, struggling to train. He understands all that and manages it in the best way. As you're grateful when you return, you give more to him than you would give under normal conditions. One thing is for someone to do their work, to comply with what people ask you to do, another thing is to have pleasure in doing so. With Mourinho, we were glad, and that doubled our performance, because one thing is to work as an obligation, another thing is to do it with joy and pleasure. He could make the player feel important and that's the secret.

Effective leaders, those who understand this concept about leadership, recognize their interdependence with regard to the environment

and work interactively with this environment in a world of possibilities. Mourinho is someone who is among his own, who is part of
them, who mingles with them. The importance of being this way is
essential. The leader is only a leader because he has followers, and he
only has followers because there are people who decide and agree to
follow. Therefore, leadership is a relationship that implies previous
choices: the choice to lead and the choice to accept leadership. Once
these two conditions are accepted, the relationship is like a candle
flame: without oxygen, it goes off.

Oxygen is precisely in the actions and attitudes of the leader.
Actions keep the flame alive, make people want to join or escape the
leader, make them remember or forget, make them want to be there or
not. Therefore, addressing the issue of leadership without taking into
account the quality of the relationship between the leader and the followers is to miss the heart of the matter. The leader's strategic positioning over his followers is critical to establish this primordial relationship
– which lives on affections, above all –which will sustain leadership.
Hence, as I said, Mourinho's positioning is essential in order for him
to be the kind of leader he is.

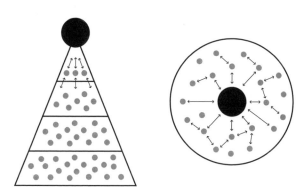

As I stated, he is positioned in the centre of the circle, not at the
top of the pyramid, as some argue it should be even today. (Desenho
com estes tipo de liderança mais a capa do Liderança) José Mourinho
is in the centre of the circle, with his own, thus establishing the
special relationships that are acknowledged (complicity, solidarity,

camaraderie, co-responsibility, among many others). John Terry said: *"When not in front of the cameras, he is one of us, part of the gang."*

In a more conversational, but no less eloquent tone for what I intend to prove here, Benny McCarthy, a South-African player, with whom Mourinho won one Champions League with FC Porto said: *"He's more of an extra-player than a coach. That's what makes him Great."* In a little deeper analysis, Vítor Baía told me:

> *He keeps a very close relationship with all those who work with him, but at the same time, there is no doubt that he is the key figure of our group. We know that he's calling the shots but, above all, we know that he is the person we trust in. Why? Because the message he conveys is one of confidence and we, as players, were always sure that if we are in a delicate situation, we'll always have someone to guide us, so that we can overcome the obstacles.*

Baía's last part of the speech is curious. This is the way the current leader frames Mourinho's position with regard to his group: *"If we were in a delicate position, we would always have someone that would know how to guide us."* Besides, isn't guiding the leader's key task?

Jorge Costa is also not far from Baía's idea as we can see:

> *He has the ability – which isn't easy – to know how to manage every situation very well. In certain moments, he's almost like a teammate and his relationship with the players is completely different from the one he has with those who aren't part of the workgroup. Herein lies his great asset or, perhaps, other coaches' great difficulty, of almost having two faces. That 'I am the Greatest' arrogant image he shows – puts him clearly at the top of the pyramid regarding the outside. He's totally different regarding his players; his speech is soft, easy and natural, and makes us believe in everything that he thinks is important, in a simple, natural way. In this case, his image is of a leader in the centre of the circle with his own. The image he projects to the outside has to do with the shield he wants his workgroup to have. However, he's almost completely open with the workgroup, he's completely in the centre of the group, and everything revolves around his ideas. I want*

*to emphasize that he doesn't impose it in any way; it's perfectly natural
and even informal.*

Didier Drogba talks about protection, but not always and at all
costs. Mourinho can also be tough when he wants to, and when he
thinks it's necessary.

> *He's very protective. He protects the workgroup as much as he can,
> and he thinks of it as family. He speaks in the first person a lot in order
> to protect his group. That's the reason why he never criticizes a player in
> front of journalists. If we lose, he tries to make excuses for us, but when
> we're in the dressing room, we better run. In that moment, he knows
> how to be tough on the players. In the end, the important thing is to
> preserve the group from outside threats, but he's not unique that way;
> basically, all coaches try to do this.*

Lastly, another example that defines and reinforces everything
that has been said – it is particularly important, because it comes
from another country with a very different culture from Portugal –
here's a description of Ian Wright, the former England international,
who made this profile after having seen Mourinho celebrating a victory with Chelsea players: *"If any other coach hugged his players, they
would freeze or shrink instinctively, surprised or embarrassed, [but with
Mourinho] the camaraderie that exists between him and the team is plain
to see."* (Ian Wright *in* Barclay 2005: 151).

This camaraderie was also evident at the end of the qualifying
round with Barcelona during the 2004/05 season, in which Chelsea
emerged victorious. Mourinho entered the pitch to celebrate and
pounced on John Terry's back, an attitude that Desmond Morris[13]
commented, as reported by Barclay (2006:150-1): *"It was this keen
observer of the human race (and hopeless football fan) Desmond Morris
who drew my attention to it. 'I can't think of another coach who had
been able to do that,' he added (...). Mourinho had both legs in the air.*

---

[13] British zoologist and ethologist who focused his studies on animal and human behaviour,
author of the bestseller The Naked Ape.

It was a body language expression that I had never seen in football.' It means he's one of the players." At another time, Morris had already said: *"I disagree slightly with the portrayal of Mourinho as a father figure to his players. He is more like an elder brother. Or the leader of the gang."* (Morris in Batty 2006:150)

Clearly, Mourinho is another element of the group. With different duties, of course, but another element. That position gives his leadership legitimacy, gives him soft power to guide, rather then hard power to command. Mourinho is a leader at the centre of the circle and not at the top of the pyramid. Therefore, by establishing relationships – long lasting relationships – his examples and leadership remain, as we can see by the influence, that he still has on men like Jorge Costa and Vítor Baía.

By the way, I can't resist the urge to leave an example that clarifies what I have just written, although in the opposite direction. It's an example that illustrates how leadership can be ephemeral, if it's not based on consistent and effective relationships. It shows what happens, if the followers don't feel free to express opinions and emotions, if they don't have a "healthy disrespect" for the leader, and if leadership is not freely and spontaneously accepted.

"As noted by President George Bush senior, when asked what had changed since he left office: 'Well, for starters, I no longer win every golf game in which I participate...'"[14]

Of course, the lines above are merely an example. Maybe George Bush senior attempted to parody the question that he had been asked, and therefore, the matter of winning or losing golf games is not even important. However, it expresses a very clear and simple idea. Faced with a certain kind of "leader", the attitudes of the followers can often be of flattery or fear (hence Bush won every game as president, but not due to the quality of his swing). When that "leader" ceases to be so, the negative feelings disappear and the sense of freedom to act or think as people see fit naturally emerges. They feel free to win golf games. What I want to enhance with this example (without questioning

[14] Kets the Vries in Como o líder pensa, (p. 68)

George Bush senior's leadership qualities), is the previously described idea that only by genuine will – for freedom, if we wish – can leadership made of voluntary acceptance endure. Mourinho's leadership fits this idea perfectly.

PASSION

We may affirm absolutely that nothing great in the world has been accomplished without passion.

(HEGEL: WWW.FAMOUS-QUOTES-AND-QUOTATIONS.COM/FAMOUS-QUOTATIONS.HTML)

In a lecture I gave about Mourinho's leadership, in which Mourinho himself was present, both of us made ourselves available to answer all the questions from the audience. The question that struck me the most came from a senior executive from Portugal Telecom, *"Congratulations, I really enjoyed everything you said. I agree with everything, but I have a question that wasn't dealt with in this session: what is the role of passion in all of this?"*

The question was addressed to me. Knowing José Mourinho, it wasn't difficult to answer. But the damage was done: the omission of something as important as passion in successful leadership. This omission will not happen here. I have learned my lesson. What is right under our nose is precisely what we can't see. Mourinho's passion for the game stands out from his childhood. It's the most visible thing we can see in his life and actions. It was exactly what I missed...

Relationships are always related to the personality of whom we are talking about. A personality that results in behaviours, ways of being and analyzing life, that reflect in the way we relate to others and even to ourselves.

I will not make an exhaustive description of the Theory of Personality Traits – because it's outdated – , however, at this stage, it's important to remember some of Mourinho's personality traits so we can understand him as a man, a manager and a leader.

First of all, there is *Passion*. Peter F. Drucker said that he never saw *"results being achieved without passion."* Frances Hesselbein, President of the Board of Directors of the Peter F. Drucker Foundation wrote that: "*the future belongs to the leaders who are passionate and courageous, who can give advice and take risks*". I couldn't agree more with both of them, but I would make a small addendum regarding Hesselbein's idea. Passion (the passionate leader, using her terminology) is the basis of all the attributes that come afterwards. I don't believe that someone without passion can give advice, be brave or even be willing to take risks, because passion involves us body and soul in the project, due to its eruptive, impetuous and stormy character. Being in love is to devote oneself to the other, because the core of passion is the *other...* whom we try to attract, to thrill or to conquer to a common project.

In many ways, passion has to do with the future. Only those who feel passion, who fall in love, are able to think in terms of the future, and are able to project themselves in it. Having passion is being able to see possibilities and thinking we can reach them; passion is not sleeping and getting up early in the morning, because of projects to be completed. To have passion is to have insight and the more passionate we are about this vision, the clearer and more ambitious it will become. Being in love, having passion, means to dream, to let your thoughts flow and to let the present fly into the future we envisage for ourselves and for others. Other than children, I don't know of anyone who has bigger dreams. That's why, when you ask them – the question itself is indicative of this reality – what they would like to be when they grow up, they always have an answer. It may be different for everyone, but they always have one: superhero, astronaut, fireman, or even a pirate. For children, the possibilities are endless and these possibilities usually lead them to occupations surrounded by an always-romantic aura. Being a child is, by definition, being in love, living with passion, living in the future and in their dream. Can there be a wider vision?

Thus, ultimately, passion provokes us and builds within us a desire for a deeper involvement in what we are doing, or want to do. Involvement is the keyword for success, and a successful leadership.

We asked Vítor Baía about the importance of passion in Mourinho, and the groups he leads. The answer was illuminating:

He's a workaholic. The only reason he doesn't work 24/7 is because he has a family, and he has to sleep, otherwise he would do just that. So, apart from sleeping and being with his family, he's always working, programming/anticipating... Players can feel his great passion perfectly. Moreover, that's part of his intrinsic qualities. Besides, those who don't have that passion can't do everything he does so naturally.

Didier Drogba also spoke to me about this subject. He showed me the separation between passion and unbridled eagerness to win. Oddly enough, Drogba directs this idea of passion for the game itself, rather than winning. He explains the meaning of the concept, and frames it in the subject of Mourinho's leadership.

Passion is a fantastic characteristic of his. He breathes, eats, and sleeps football. It's football at all times. But he knows how to separate things, and that's what I like about him. Football is one thing, winning is something else. He used to tell us: 'If we play well today and we give our best, even if defeat is the end result, we can have dinner, reassured and with a clear conscience.' However, if we don't play our best, life with him becomes difficult.

And this way of being comes from his passion for the game?

Partly, yes. You know, to be a great football coach, you need to have a great passion for the game, no matter whom we are speaking of. Why? Because football is a passion of mine, and of his as well. Look, I don't think there are many coaches out there that were midfielders in the Portuguese third division, and who have reached as far as he did. It takes a lot of passion to do what he does, for sure.

Lastly, it would be interesting to look at the word's etymology. Passion, from the Latin *passio*, means *to endure, and suffer*; we are here faced with the perennial nature of passion. If we look closely at Mourinho's most common procedures, his involvement, his ability to always be "in the game", his insatiable competitiveness, his ambition and constant focus on winning, among others, we can easily find features of tremendous passion for his job and for the game.

LOSING IS NOT AN OPTION

He [Mourinho] had infected us with the victory virus, the desire to always win. Only success mattered. (DROGBA, 2009: 154)

Another personality trait arising in Mourinho (apart from his enduring and untiring enchantment, and from his passion) is his thirst for victory. For Mourinho, "losing is not an option".

In this regard, Jorge Costa remembers his arrival at FC Porto quite well and revealed to me that with Mourinho...

From the first day we started working, victory is on everybody's mind and on the tip of everyone's tongue. When I say 'first day' I mean just that, because this idea, this spirit of victory, enters us like a kind of seed, whose fruit we'll reap later. And the truth is we would play at Sporting Lisbon, Manchester United, Barcelona, and our sole idea was that we were going to win, because we knew and felt we could win. We were completely convinced that we were the best, and we really were. The truth is that we won every match, both in Portugal and in Europe.

Similarly, Vítor Baía emphasizes the virtues of this attitude of victory:

He is perfectly focused on victory, hooked on it, I would even say. In this respect, he's quite clear in his objectives and leaves no room for doubts to anybody for the only thing he wants: to win. To achieve this, his message of confidence for us is quite strong. Beyond this confidence he conveyed us, we felt we were the world's best players. We may not have been, but in our hearts we felt we were.

Finally, my own testimony. Of course, I'm thrilled by Mourinho's victories and suffer with his defeats. I often congratulate him when he accomplishes an important victory. Whenever I do so, Mourinho's tendency is to devalue what he has just won and to focus on what he has yet to win. One example happened the day before I wrote this. Mourinho had just been considered the best manager in

Italy for the 2008/09 season. I congratulated him, and he immediately replied: *"Thanks, but what matters is to win the championship. That is what's important."*

I also remember another example that illustrates this successful way of being, in which only victory matters. An episode that demonstrates this philosophy, but at the same time, tells us how to win: you can only win… by intrinsically believing you can win. At the end of the first-leg of the Champions League semi-final with Deportivo La Coruna at Estádio das Antas, I waited for Mourinho outside FC Porto's dressing room and we went to dinner. It was almost midnight. The game had ended goalless, which meant that the match in Spain would be extremely difficult. Even more so, during that season, Deportivo "had trashed" all their opponents at Riazor stadium (e.g., AC Milan had "suffered" four goals in the previous round). Thus, the outlook was very unattractive for the match that would decide whether or not FC Porto would go to the final. I was devastated, I must confess. I had doubts that Mourinho's team managed to go to La Coruna to win or even draw by more than two goals. The trip to the restaurant was kind of quiet, the only words exchanged were small talk. Witnessing Mourinho's supreme calmness in the restaurant, I said: *"Zé, Deportivo played better. It will be terrible over there. We're screwed."* Undisturbed, Mourinho continued to spread butter on his bread and, without even looking at me, he said, *"Don't worry. I'll beat them up."* He started to chew his piece of bread until he finally looked at me. I replied: "Whatever you say", and immediately thought to myself: he will beat them up?!? Just like that? After they just gave him a beating, he's going there to beat them up? Is this bloke crazy or senseless?

I never forgot this episode, especially because two weeks later, FC Porto went to Coruña to "beat them up": they won 1-0 and qualified for the final.

When I asked what else Didier Drogba remembered from the time he worked with Mourinho, the answer was the idea of victory and confidence in achieving it:

First of all, I remember his winning attitude. He's a winner, without a shadow of a doubt. And one becomes a leader because he knows

---

what he's doing and how he makes others believe in what he's doing. If anyone attends a training session with doubts, not quite knowing what to do, confused, very emotional, he ends up losing control and then nothing works. So you have to be confident in what you're doing. José Mourinho is confident in what he does and he conveys it.

THE GUIDED DISCOVERY

"Discovery consists of seeing what everybody has seen and thinking what nobody has thought." (ANONYMOUS IN THOMAS, 2009: 103)

I have already spoken about José Mourinho's idea of leadership. His definition is easy to remember: *"What is leadership? For me, leadership is to guide, rather than issuing commands."*

The methodology that shapes Mourinho's entire work, especially as a coach and as a leader, resides precisely in this way of thinking. Mourinho dubbed this methodology *Guided Discovery*. Let us see how he defined it in his 2003 biography, written by me:

My Guided Discovery has more to do with feeling, rather than noticing, i.e., how the players feel in a particular situation or movement. I ask them what they feel during an experimentation... let's see how this position feels as you have support... On a mental level, I'm not afraid of making mistakes, because this is covered... This is how we start. We work it out during training and I get feedback that allows me to change according to that. I have that elasticity, that ability to make changes within the exercise according to what they tell me. If what they tell me makes me realize the exercise is not appropriate for the situation, I'll change it immediately. Sometimes, after three minutes, I have already introduced a new rule to the exercise, in order to adapt it to what the players are feeling. Deep down, this operation is directly connected to the Guided Discovery.

This methodology contains a multitude of ideas. A thousand pages wouldn't be enough to describe the wealth of this statement, but that's not our goal. However, this isn't possible, or desirable here. Here are a few considerations that I think are essential.

First of all, *Guided Discovery* is a key factor in modern organizations: it stimulates mental efficiency. By discussing, questioning, and experimenting, *Guided Discovery* requires the employee to think/feel – and because this is not just any brainstorming where all reasoning is allowed - the player is encouraged to think effectively towards framing the questions that arise; he must also evolve for himself, because it's an evolutionary process and everyone must follow it. Whoever stops thinking will be left behind and will not be able to progress with the others.

By questioning and experimenting, Mourinho's method does not allow stagnation. It's always evolving in a joint process of evolution where everyone participates; nothing is the same today as it was yesterday. Those who abandon that route are left behind and that eradicates any chance of *group thinking*. I call your attention to the relevance of the disagreement; it may be interesting to cite an instructive example we can read in the book *A Essência da Liderança* by Arménio Rego and Pina e Cunha, quoting the November, 1999 edition of "Fortune" magazine:

> *The relevance of the disagreement is symbolized in an episode usually attributed to Alfred Sloan, GM's legendary president, serving for a quarter of a century. (...) At a meeting with his "general staff", Sloan raised this simple question: 'Gentlemen, it appears we fully agree with this decision, am I right?' As he saw everybody nodding in approval, he said: 'Therefore, I propose we suspend the definitive analysis of this matter until the next meeting, so we can have time to discover any contradiction and perhaps be able to better understand what this decision means.'*

Let me cite one more repeated statements of Western democracies: "*From discussion springs light.*" Indeed we have evolved through a clash of ideas, through the exchange of arguments, through the analysis of the facts, through continued experimentation, both as human beings and as organizations, because the various perspectives, even when seen as antagonistic, are integral facets of the same reality, of which each has their own vision. I would risk saying that a coin does not have only two sides. Paradoxically, it has three sides; the third is the "whole" which is the coin itself, which we often tend to forget.

This is how we reach the state of homeostasis as we grow, change, and evolve. In an apparent paradox, the action and the resulting transformation reaches the dynamic balance that allows us to continue the ongoing process of evolution / transformation through action.

One of the main foundations of Mourinho's *Guided Discovery* is found here. The teams coached by José Mourinho evolve, transform themselves daily in a naturally balanced way.

Another return is the natural feedback, as an increasingly necessary factor for the development of organizations. Through the feedback resulting from practice, the system is corrected and improved, as it tries to surpass itself. And Mourinho has been accomplishing this in an irreproachable manner.

But we're not done yet. Guided Discovery provokes and leads to people – meaning the players – getting involved. And this is every leaders' dream. Napoleon defined a leader as "a merchant of hope", which is to say a manager of expectations. This negotiation requires everyone's involvement. *Guided Discovery* creates this involvement by bringing people into the discussion, making them participate in their own future, making them find a path for the group, making them decide and comment on their own comfort and most effective way to perform their tasks.

This vital involvement by the employees in the organizations and their projects is clear in the words of Vítor Baía, when confronted with Mourinho's *Guided Discovery*:

> *Players like to feel important. If you don't give them a sense of importance, problems will arise, sooner or later. With Mourinho, the players felt important, because due to the Guided Discovery, we got involved in the process, but it was a global involvement, from the so-called superstars to the kids fresh from the junior team. On the other hand, this full involvement facilitated – and how – the emergence,*

development and consolidation of the much-talked about group spirit in FC Porto.

Focusing his relationship with Mourinho in the old maxim "different among equals", Deco's words prove such a need for the player to be involved and to feel important within the group.

> *I think he managed to get the best out of me in various aspects. First of all, he built a fantastic team; when we're in a team that plays well, works well and that has a superior quality, things flow much better. Then, he knew exactly how to make me feel important within the team without differentiating me from the others; this way he could make me play at the maximum level of my abilities.*

Admittedly, when we talk about *Guided Discovery*, the goal has been envisioned, and Mourinho has a global idea of the route he wants to trace – that's why he's the leader. However, you make the path by walking, and we can only see the whole path after we crossed it. Nowadays, there are no black and white paths, and endless crossroads compel us to correct the course constantly. Therein lies the crucial importance of *Guided Discovery*. Mourinho already knows where he wants to go, he just doesn't know whether or not he can use his previously outlined path. I would even say he'll have a great difficulty in doing so, and will succeed only sporadically.

I'll transcribe Gustavo Pires in *Agôn – Gestão de Desporto* (p.140), in his interpretation of the book *Managing Chaos* (1992), by Ralph Stacey:

> *(...) the dominating thought leads managers to think they have to design the ideal map before embarking on the task of building the future. Common sense dictates that, before you start, you need to know where to go and have some idea of how to get there, but most of the maps in use today no longer meet the needs of our ever-changing times. Those maps were designed in response to a bygone world. According to Stacey, the idea that a map can be drawn a priori in turbulent times is a fantasy without a practical application. The path and destination*

must be discovered during the journey itself. You must constantly design new maps if indeed you wish to build something. The key to success is creativity; to be able to make new maps that really address the needs of the organization in the future.

This is the type of involvement Mourinho wants, one with creativity, where the future is uncertain and changes every day. Hence, Vítor Baía's words when I interviewed him for this book:

I haven't been with him since 2004, but I'm certain if I were to train with him now, he would be a completely different coach. He's always changing when it comes to training. Let me give you an example: imagine a coach who was champion in a given year by using certain methods. That coach probably thinks that next year he should follow the same methods that led him to win the championship the year before. It's a mistake! Things evolve, and whoever thinks that way – unfortunately we have coaches like that, who should do a refreshing on this matter – is making a huge mistake, and is completely out of touch with reality. Going back to José Mourinho, I'm sure that after 4 or 5 years he's not the same; only because he pushes himself, compels himself to evolve, to look for new solutions, new methods, new strategies, etc., to adapt himself to the evolution of things. So if I attended one of his training sessions and noticed that he hadn't changed, that would be the biggest disappointment of my life, because it would mean that I didn't know him as well as I thought. However, I'm sure he's different and he has evolved. In fact, look at his move from FC Porto to Chelsea. He got there, saw a completely different reality from FC Porto, he adapted and learned to benefit from players with a completely different culture from ours. Now that he got to Inter, what he does is no longer the same he did in England because, once again, the reality of Inter is quite different. The strategies that Mourinho uses now have nothing to do with his previous ones at Chelsea or FC Porto.

Guided Discovery also enables an atmosphere of trust. It is almost needless to recall the value of the concept of trust when referring to areas such as human relations (inside and outside of organizations) whatever their nature might be. Without the trust of his followers, no leader can lead, or even be able to draw some sort of extraordinary achievement from anyone. Hence, *Guided Discovery* assumes a paramount role in the matter of trust, especially from the standpoint of the leader himself. When I trust, I make people trust me, and the leader has to be the example. It is worth to quote the dialogue I had with Jorge Costa on this subject:

How do you see the results of this process [Guided Discovery] today? In fact, that's the involvement in the project, and the greater the involvement is, the greater the dedication will be, and the results will be probably better...

It is the old issue: if we're told to do something, we do it! But, if someone suggests we do it, we'll find obstacles here and there and we'll have to find the way, and I think we grow more easily and more effectively. I usually give this example: which national team was one of the best in the world and won so much? The Soviet Union based on Dynamo Kiev that was a football-playing machine. They had everything finely tuned and their football resembled geometry. However, from a certain point on, people started observing the matches and the opposing teams started realizing how they played. From that moment on, they never won anything again! That's why I find very interesting that we make mistakes and learn from our mistakes so we can grow up. This kind of growth is different from just being told what to do. If we go into a match without understanding its fundamentals, or the logic of what we're doing, we won't know how to react, and we'll fail when something unexpected happens.

But is it usual for managers to act that way? Asking opinions and raising the debate with the players?

It's not easy, because they think that by doing so, they may lose authority within the group. No, it's not easy for a manager to discuss ideas with the players.

So, José Mourinho is a professional who is comfortable in his role as a manager and has no problems asking for the opinion of those who work with him?!...

... and he likes to know our opinion; he doesn't lose sight of his ideas, but enjoys knowing other opinions. We can't forget that today, the football player is already an evolved professional with his own ideas.

José Mourinho asks questions, demands participation, opinions, and wants to improve with everyone's participation. Asking and listening to his players giving their opinion on how to play do not intimidate him. Why? Because he trusts them, and in addition to obtaining positive practical results – the improvement of team play – he also earns the confidence of his players. José Mourinho is the first to trust, to create the environment for dialogue and a space for opinion, of mutual trust, because everyone contributes, directly and effectively, for the common purpose, which is to improve in order to win. We are in a knowledgeable society, and its representative is the Human Being, what Peter F. Drucker dubbed "the educated person". I see no reason why the football world can't be along with all the other worlds – economic, political, social, etc., – deeply associated with the new realities of this "knowledgeable society".

This notion is closely connected to another one: by what was said above, we now understand that Mourinho just wants intelligent and culturally evolved players for his teams.

There was one sentence that caught my attention in Didier Drogba's autobiography:

Mourinho is not a coach who trains players. He chooses people who are prepared to adhere to his philosophy. And most importantly, they are not necessarily the best players in the world. (DROGBA, 2008: 152)

Two years later, at Chelsea's training ground in England, I asked Didier what he meant by this statement.

Well, he doesn't teach me how to play football. I know how to play football. He teaches me how to play in a team, which is something different. And that's why he's successful, wherever he is. He's not like Arsène Wenger, for example, who wants a player to grow with him. Mourinho wants mature players, or close to maturity, so he doesn't have to spend time on major technical issues. That's why he only likes intelligent players, who possess the conditions to easily grasp the intended tactical culture. When we're in the game we don't have time to think, we make split-second decisions. That's why I say the player must be able to absorb his game philosophy, and that's what I've learned from him.

That's why he can build the best team in the world without having the world's best players, as you say...

You see, who was I, who was John Terry, Frank Lampard, Arjen Robben or Damien Duff when Mourinho arrived at Chelsea? We weren't the best nor even world renowned players. We reached the group of the best with him. We all had the potential to reach the top, but we weren't there yet. With his help, we improved our capabilities a lot in a very short time, and today we're considered part of the group of the best. This happened because he managed to bring out all that potential in us.

With Mourinho, the player plays with his head as much or more than with his feet. The player must understand the fundamentals, the basics of the game; he has to participate, give opinions and debate. His football starts in his head, in the way he understands the game, how he learns it, and how he evolves. *Guided Discovery* is, unequivocally, the best tool for this development. In his interview, Vítor Baía was instructive at some point of our talk: "*He raised dialogue and discussions to know, or try to know, what was on our mind, and then he would decide according to everyone.*"

As Fritjof Capra said – referred to above, in another context – in *The Hidden Connections: a Science for Sustainable Living* (New York, 2002, Harper Collins, p. 122), it is up to the leader to enable the process of emergency – "creating novelty" – and thereby promote creativity: "*This means creating conditions – instead of giving orders – and using the power of authority to empower others.*" The creation of conditions that enable the emergence imply, according to Capra, "*building an active communication network with multiple feedback circuits*", in order to develop a culture "*open to new ideas and new knowledge*" in which "*continuous questioning is encouraged and innovation is rewarded.*"

Herein lies the result of *Guided Discovery*: the encouragement of the discussion process (trial and error) follows the natural emergence of new solutions, new processes and new methods in Mourinho's groups.

Finally, the theoretical framework of *Guided Discovery*, conceptualized in what many scholars consider to be the four activities of knowledge management of any organization:

Information capture (both individual and collective) that consists in an organization / management being prepared (in terms of knowledge) whenever a member of his team leaves or is transferred to another company;

Creation of Ideas, since all employees should be encouraged to present new ideas through their analysis of their organization;

Information Storage, i.e., the information collected is organized so that everyone can use it whenever they need;

Distribution of Information, since information is historically regarded as a source of power, the organization must make sure that it reaches everyone.

Within this framework, it is not difficult for us to understand how *Guided Discovery* fits the modern theories of management and information management. It is really the information flowing naturally through its elements, in order to generate knowledge, which is perhaps the safest and most effective capital of modern organizations.

I would like to end this subject with a story that, I believe, may help us think about the way we can achieve our goals. Most of the times we tend to complicate things. Basically, Mourinho's formula is the simplest I know: he asks questions and asks for help to those who are on the pitch about the best and most effective way one can play football.

Regarding simplicity, let us see one final example: Casanova, the famous lover, was on his deathbed when someone knocked on his door, repeatedly asking to speak with him. Casanova's doctor replied that it would be impossible, given his patient's critical state. Only his closest relatives could see him. When he heard the noise outside, Casanova learned about what was going on and gave orders to let such an insistent character in. He would have something important to tell him, for sure. When he finally came in, the young man said: *"Mr. Casanova, you made love to over twelve hundred of the most beautiful Italian women..."* Casanova interrupted him. *"Fifteen hundred."* *"Okay, okay. Fifteen hundred of the most beautiful women of our country. But how did you do it? You must tell me your secret."* Casanova signalled at him to come closer, winked conspiratorially, and whispered in his ear: *"I asked them."*

MOTIVATION

Il [Mourinho] nous a donné soif. La soif de la victoire. Il était impensable de remporter ces trophées avant son arrivée. Quelles victoires! Quelles experiences! Quelle succession de rencontres avec une équipe qui en voulait! Nous avons gravi jour après jour les marches nous menant vers la grand victoire du championnat. Nous voilà habités par une volonté indescriptible de tout rafler. (...) Il m'a enseigné la rage de vaincre. (GALLAS[15], KELLY, 2008: 95-98)

With FC Porto, before an important match between Porto and Benfica, Mourinho came upon an interview of Manuel Vilarinho (then Benfica's President), who claimed to have dreamed that his team would win 3-0 at Estádio das Antas.

When Vilarinho made his dream public, I immediately thought: 'There's the provocation I need to stir my players' pride.' I immediately made a copy of the interview of Benfica's president and placed it on the dressing room wall all week long, so that no one would forget Vilarinho's dream. I told the newspapers that nobody beats us 3-0 at home. And we went to the match somewhat heckled.

(LOURENÇO 2004: 105)

The truth is the match ended with a 3-2 victory for FC Porto.

---

[15] William Gallas, French international who played for Chelsea when Mourinho arrived at the English club.

Before I present Mourinho as a leader, by introducing some background in the theories of leadership, let me give you one last (purely pragmatic) look at one of his personality traits I find most outstanding: his capacity to motivate.

The word motivation is closely related to two other words that reflect the underlying concept well, once intertwined: *motive and action*. Wikipedia defines it as "*an inner strength that changes throughout life, which directs and enhances the goals of an individual.*" In real life, this is about something we look for and act, move toward the accomplishment of that goal, of that something we seek. The reason for doing something can be either internal or external. As Robin Sieger writes in *Vencedores Natos, Como atingir a realização Pessoal* (Sieger, 2005, p. 215-16):

> *Identify what motivates you. Your internal motivation will be your incentive to change. Internal motivation can be very powerful if it's a deeply felt commitment, resulting from your goal-setting and passion.*
>
> *A group of people decides to quit drinking alcohol during January; those who do it successfully once can do it every year, because they are internally committed to do it. External motivation is equally powerful; few things are more likely to make you stop drinking than hearing your doctor say your liver will suffer if you don't.*

After this short introduction, let us read Mourinho's words from where his capacity to motivate comes, in structural terms. What the engine, or the source if you will, for all his motivation is:

> *I think the best way to motivate – at least, the more consistent, less doubtful, easier to understand, and of greater durability – is to motivate others with my own motivations. I started that way, and I'll end up that way. I think my own motivations are the best engine of motivations for the ones I lead. I want to win, to be the best, to win collective but also individual prizes, I want to add Cup after Cup, to get the best contract, make more money, to better prepare my family's future, to be historically recognized as the best or one of the best, to leave a mark*

wherever I go, and that the supporters of the clubs where I have been remember me as someone important. These are some of my – many – motivations I naturally pass to all those who work with me on the way I talk, act, behave, gesture, and put pressure on every minute of every day. Therefore, I consider my motivation to be the key to the motivation of others, because mine is directly linked to the others and their own motivations. For example, I want the medical department to also have the ambition to be better every day, to beat records, and in this particular case, I'll never forget Derlei's recovery at FC Porto. He had surgery in December, and everyone over there said he would never play again that season. Later – far from thinking he would get there – I said I wanted him to play in the Champions League final. When things began to rush towards the final, Derlei himself said that he would play in the semi-final, rather than the final. Thus a wave of motivation towards a goal was created. Everyone in the club committed themselves in an absolutely amazing way. In fact, he ended up playing in one of the semi-final matches (his goal in Corunna qualified us for the final) and in the final. And this happened because, in my opinion, there was a general motivation: mine, Derlei's, of the medical department (surgeon, masseur, etc.), the fitness trainer's; even in his own home, with his wife getting involved, and also being an important source of motivation to him. A lot of us embraced a motivation, a purpose. I think that, deep down, it's the leader's motivation that endures. Personally, this intrinsic motivation is like breathing. It's part of us, and the day that I stop breathing it's because I died. Well, that's what will happen to me in my profession. The day I lose motivation is because I'm professionally dead. In other words, the day I lack motivation means it's time to pack it in and leave football.

When I asked Vítor Baía about Mourinho's motivation his reply was enlightening, it seemed to have been agreed upon. I smiled, I heard Baía and now I quote, verbatim, with all the redundancies in which the spoken language sometimes skids, purposefully, so that everyone realizes the worth and impact of the message when it's genuine, as the question of motivation in José Mourinho is: "*It has to do with him, it's intrinsic... it's his, its the person, and we feel that, we all felt it. It has to do with him, how he puts all of his convictions in practice!"* Therefore, Baía believes that, in terms of motivation, Mourinho is unique in his ability to convey a strong desire to win and in the intensity of this ambition: *"We felt it so completely, and we felt it the year after his departure from FC Porto... We had won the UEFA Cup and had been European champions; after that, we clearly felt the balloon losing air. People were different, the message was different..."*

In another reasoning, Jorge Costa concludes that Mourinho's self-motivation is genuine. He strongly believes in what he says, which is why he always ends up influencing / motivating his followers:

> *Basically, Mourinho's motivation is connected to the speech he gives to the outside. Obviously, a coach, whoever he might be, always tells his players they're the best, that all matches must be won, etc. In other words, I don't think there is a single manager who goes to play at Porto, at Benfica, at Sporting Lisbon or at Manchester United and tells his players that he wants to lose by few points. But it seems to me, there are very few who say and assume they're going to win the way Mourinho does. He is always adamant and everyone always knows what he means: 'I'm going to win, I have the best team and the best players...' To say this publicly, the way he does it, you have to be very brave, have tons of confidence, and be a little 'crazy', even. Except all of this has a highly positive effect on the players. All of his public commitments – let me remind you of assertions such as 'Next year, we'll be champions' when he arrived at FC Porto, or his reaction to fans, players and opponents, in defeat, at home, with Panathinaikos when he said 'we'll win over there' – also remember that, at home, the Greek team had been unbeaten in the UEFA Cup for two and a half years – motivate the players completely. When a coach says that neither the opponent nor the stadium matter, because he's there to win, he has a whole different speech from a coach who says he believes, he expects to win, but... maybe... The speeches are utterly different. The latter coach doesn't commit to a victory, nor compromises his players. In José Mourinho's case, the coach is committing himself, saying that his players are the best. Therefore, the players are automatically committed to*

their leader who's sticking his neck out for them. This speech is indeed a very important motivation factor, because the players start to believe and have no doubts that they are the best, and they will win no matter where they are.

Through his intent, Mourinho co-creates his own reality which, in turn, is embodied in a victory.

And after listening to Vítor Baía, I cannot resist quoting Sieger again, as a complement to what was stated:

Our plan is part of the process of our future success. Having self-confidence, acting coherently and being firmly convinced that we will win is equally important. This means that the plan is not just something we say or write: it's something we embody 24/7 hours a day.

(SIEGER 2005: 115)

Here, we have a description of what Mourinho considers his structural way to motivate his players. Everything is genuine nothing is artificial. The most important thing in Man is the emotion, and not the thought. Reality is carried out from the heart, not from reason. Hence, Didier Drogba finds it difficult to explain this topic.

It's hard to explain. There are situations that have to be experienced to be fully understood. We must 'be inside' to understand them. He instilled a spirit of conquest in us. Only victory mattered because he convinced us we were the best, even if we weren't. With each passing day, our confidence grew stronger, sturdier, and more consistent. But, like I said, it's very difficult to explain, only by living and feeling the moment, living and feeling his whole game philosophy that requires a certain team spirit. Naturally, when we work as a team we need to have team spirit; but with Mourinho, this is the whole point.

Mourinho is like that, a naturally driven man; in such a way and with such consistency that he passes his motivation on to his players, by way of his speech, his presence, and his body language. Hence, motivation is one of the most consistent features of his leadership. To lead is to influence and when the influence is so natural and decisive in terms of motivation, as it is in José Mourinho's case, the results can only be superior.

Deco illustrates how Mourinho's motivation managed to yield exceptional psychological results. Mourinho managed to "free" Porto's players, breaking psychological barriers, showing them that the limit would only be found through victory.

In fact, Mourinho came to break an already existing barrier. Indeed, Porto had already won a European Champions Cup, but that was a long time ago. When Mourinho arrived there, FC Porto had not yet taken the leap by European standards. They had often reached the quarterfinals but, from then on, something blocked the players and unconsciously, they thought it would be nearly impossible to go further and compete with teams that had history and a far superior financial capacity. Mourinho broke that, somehow; hence the UEFA Cup victory was very important for us, because it gave us an incredible sense of confidence...

Some players said they considered themselves invincible. Was that it?

I wouldn't say invincible. It was more feeling such a confidence that, while respecting our opponents, we knew that we could dispute the match with anyone and win. I usually say – and that's why I went to Barcelona – that a player feels big because of where he is, because of which team he plays in. If I'm in Barcelona, or in Real Madrid, etc., I naturally feel I can win over anyone. That was what was missing in Porto until Mourinho arrived. There was always that last step that seemed sort of insurmountable. Mourinho put an end to that psychological barrier and, back then, we played against any team in Europe and for us it was the same because, besides being a strong team already, we were also a team with a lot of personality and a lot of self-confidence.

However, his way of motivating does not end here. In addition to the structural motivation in José Mourinho, there still is, in a profound and quite surprising way, the situational motivation – meant for a very specific case. Here too, in my opinion, Mourinho is brilliant in how he reaches, shapes, influences and motivates his players according to the moment, the situation or the obstacle. As you will see in a moment, he always does it in an inclusive manner, without separating or taking anything out of context, in yet another example of the paradigm of complexity in action.

Here are Mourinho's words, quoted from *Mourinho – Porquê tantas vitórias?* (P. 179-80):

Theoretically, the players are always naturally focused on the more important games. Before we face Real Madrid or Manchester United, I think we don't even need any kind of work on the motivational level. In those matches, the players are naturally motivated to give their best. I'm talking about theoretically more difficult matches, associated with a certain type of stress and/or pressure. It's essential for players to be able to transform this tension and pressure (their own emotions) in motivation and focus. When it comes to playing against a tough opponent, in a big arena, this is naturally achieved.

The problem occurs during theoretically easier matches, or even after the team wins several matches in a row. During such games, the motivation often becomes problematic. Imagine if Chelsea faced an opponent from the third division for the FA Cup. In these matches, players tend to be less focused, more relaxed, like when they are faced with easy exercises during training. The apparent simplicity, during the matches or in training, can lead to slackness, and that's usually when surprises happen.

One of the things I do to avoid this tendency is, the week before the match when we are preparing for it, I create situations with a high degree of difficulty, or even unenforceable, to create failure and a lack of efficacy. Thus, I can put pressure on players and leave them less confident. By accomplishing this during training with a ball, I'm forcing them to achieve a greater degree of focus later, to work harder, and to be motivated not to fail. If you start to doubt yourself, you push yourself further, so you can naturally get better results.

We can also go back to a time when Mourinho was at União de Leiria. This next example illustrates the imagination that we sometimes need to have to obtain the motivation of those who follow us. When I travel to Angola, where I continuously provide training to numerous Angolan "senior managers", and when I talk about motivation they often tell me: *"For Mourinho, it's easy to motivate. The clubs he has managed are rich. It's always easy to motivate people with monetary incentives. Our problem is that we don't have those millions..."* But Mourinho did not always manage rich clubs, and União de Leiria is a proof of that.

Let's go back to the 2001/02 season, which transported José Mourinho to a whole new reality. For the first time in his career, he chose and prepared a team (União de Leiria) from scratch. Not knowing almost any one of his players, he tried to empathize with his group right away and motivate it at the same time. To achieve his objectives, he committed himself, making it clear that his motivation was high:

> *I have no doubt that I will go to one of 'the big ones' sooner or later. When I go, some of you will go with me." Everyone was touched by the promise and the hope it contained. "I never specified who would go with me, because it would depend on the club where I was headed. I knew, for example, that Benfica needed a left-back and therefore, Nuno Valente would surely go with me. Benfica also needed a winger and Maciel also knew that, if I went to the Stadium of Light, he would go with me. They knew they would eventually go with me. This situation was a motivating factor for the players and, at the same time, it created complicity between us. Like 'you help me get there then I'll take some of you with me'. That's how I committed myself to the group..."* (MOURINHO IN LOURENÇO 2004: 86-7).

Some months later, Mourinho left União de Leiria to train "one of the big ones" – FC Porto. At the end of the season, he signed three players from his former club: Nuno Valente, Tiago and Derlei. Later on, it was time for Maciel to follow in the footsteps of his teammates.

Regarding imagination, Mourinho is often a provocatively motivator. Vilarinho's dream, mentioned earlier, was an episode for posterity.

Fitting Mourinho in Leadership Theories

An effective leader wants strong partners; he encourages them, pushes them, and is proud of them. (DRUCKER, 2008: 293)

Today, we find that current research tends to recover more ancient views on leadership, framing them in current situations. The Great Man Theory or Trait Theory from the second half of the 1940s is somehow recovered in view of the typical personality traits, only with a new backdrop. In fact, we're talking about the cult of personality that any leader can fall prey to. In José Mourinho's case, this aspect also connects to how companies like Samsung and American Express use his image to promote their products. Samsung's commercial, as previously mentioned, is instructive. Mourinho is a real James Bond, a superman, *a great man.* Just like 007, Mourinho makes common mortals dream, because we would all like to be a bit like James Bond or like Mourinho. This was probably the reasoning made by Samsung's marketing department.

What do José Mourinho and James Bond (the great men) have in common, in order to make us dream? Somehow, they predict the future, are brave, determined, bold, are competent in what they do, they face the dangers and look good, among other qualities. It would be impossible to trace all of José Mourinho's personality features that contribute to his image. Let's dwell on some of the more important ones that arise in the Samsung commercial, and we'll compare them to the Trait Theory later.

What are the most striking features of his personality, according to the commercial we are exploring? Mourinho is courageous – remember how he presented himself in his profession, facing and breaking established canons, something that earned him many wars, enemies and hatred. Mourinho is determined – for example, in the way he never deviated from the path traced by himself in his profession over the years. Mourinho is bold – he takes risks and gets exposed, as few other managers do; imagine the trouble he would've been into if he had failed in his prediction about the formation of Barcelona's team...

Mourinho is competent and the results he obtained prove it beyond a shadow of a doubt.

These attributes project a global image of Mourinho to the outside world. Within the organization where he works other attributes are recognized, such as ambition (the will to win every time), honesty, integrity (he looks in the eye, he does what he says and says what he does) and intelligence (always a step ahead of everyone else). Here are a few personality traits that constitute Mourinho's character – a sketch, if you like. All of them, integrated in the larger whole that constitutes the human being that he is, contribute to characterize Mourinho's leadership.

Besides, in the history of the study of "Leadership" this is exactly where everything began: in the relentless pursuit of the personality traits required to determine the essence of leadership. The systematic study of the subject began immediately after the end of World War II. Without any great certainty, it is believed that the studies were initiated during that time due to the emergence of great leaders during the war, both military and civilian. Anyway, these studies are very recent in academics. Therefore, there are still no answers to the various questions, everything remains unresolved, and all doubts are admissible.

Studies evolved almost contemporaneously with the study of the "Trait Theory". Two North-American universities (Ohio and Michigan) contributed to the study of behaviour as a foundation of good leadership. In other words, it didn't matter who the leader was, what he thought or what he defended. Only his behaviour was important. For them, the essence of leadership was behavioural and a framework for behaviours would be created to determine an effective leadership in any given situation.

These studies continued until the 60s, after which the Contingency theory appeared. Here, they chose the path of contextualizing the leader in his environment. The theme of effective leadership was studied as being involved in a complex relational web established amongst personality traits, behaviours, and – herein lays the next step – situational factors. The problem was studied in real life settings, precisely to try to identify the various situational conditions. The other novelty of the study arises from the fact that it is acceptable that the leader changes his leadership style according to the situation, his environment if you like:

> *The relationship between leadership style and effectiveness suggests that, under condition 'a', style 'x' may be adequate, while the style 'y' is more appropriate for the situation 'b', and style 'z' more appropriate for the situation 'c'. But what would those situations, 'a, b and c' be?*
>
> (ROBBINS 2002: 309)

The Contingency theory aimed at the pursuit of this understanding. However, all these studies have failed and were eventually abandoned for a common reason: they never managed to find a conceptual framework to determine the effectiveness of leadership in a precise and doubtless way. They also reached the conclusion that if this conceptual framework could exist in theory, it would be so extensive and complex (e.g., with regard to a human's personality traits, a study has identified 17,000[16]) that it would never prove anything. Last but not least, it was also noticed that the same traits, the same behaviours, or even identical situations, worked in certain times and places but not in others. And so, the Contingency Theory studies failed to give rise to Neocharismatic Theories in the 1980s. It is precisely the point where we are today and where I will frame José Mourinho's leadership.

NEOCHARISMATIC THEORIES

Since the 1980s, the investigation has started to focus on the leader and his traits. It was like revisiting the Trait Theory, trying to deepen it in the light of new concepts.

These theories are divided into two major blocks, according to most scholars: the Charismatic leadership and the Transformational leadership. I must say that, for a long time, I have argued that Mourinho could be seen simultaneously as a charismatic and a transformational leader. As we will see in a moment, I don't think it is essentially so, nowadays.

---

[16] Study from Allport and Odbert cited in Soto, 2001: 51)

Structurally, Neocharismatic Theories emphasize the leader's symbolic and emotionally appealing behaviours. They try to explain how leaders can lead their followers to high performances, while blurring the distance between leader and follower.

The first theory in this specific field is the Attribution Theory of Leadership, authored by J. C. McElroy, in 1982. This scientific thinking tells us that leadership is an attributed concept, not one that is won. Therefore, McElroy (1982) argues that leadership is given due to the recognition and attribution of extraordinary capabilities to someone by their followers. It sort of takes up the Trait Theory; the leader is attributed and recognized with characteristics such as intelligence, boldness and strong personality, strong verbal skills, aggressiveness, understanding, the spirit, and initiative, among many other features by their followers.

CHARISMATIC LEADERSHIP

Based on the development of the vision presented by McElroy, we arrived at the charismatic leadership. It is common today (almost mandatory, I would say) to attribute to leaders, whoever they are, the label "charismatic" and "non-charismatic", as if leadership and the leader's characteristics were limited to this.

By looking at the leader, with the distinctive personality traits they see in him, followers tend to attribute heroic or extraordinary leadership abilities to him. Then, a sort of halo appears around the leader; the followers tend to regard him as someone superior, capable of amazing feats and able to fulfil the team members' dreams.

Etymologically speaking, *charisma* is a Greek word meaning "gift of divine inspiration". Nowadays, the concept can mean an unusual ability to inspire fascination and loyalty; therefore, a leader is blindly believed, followed and is expected to guide his followers along the path that leads to the realization of the dream of each and every one. On the other hand, the so-called charismatic leaders are often described as being self-confident, grounded in firm convictions, full of energy, possessors of an enthusiastic confident and, with a particular attention to this, are people with a huge *"capacity to manipulate symbols of power and success to exert an emotional pull from their follow-ers*" (Nye Jr., 2009: 82). In this area, the empathy between leader and followers is particularly prominent, without which there is no such thing as a charismatic leadership.

Many have been considered charismatic leaders, for better or for worse, but always generating a lot of empathy. Men such as Mahatma Gandhi or Martin Luther King, Adolf Hitler or Osama bin Laden. Why? Because charisma is not just a personal attribute, an individual mark, or a character trait; charisma also derives from the relationship between leader and followers. The personality traits, the history, the followers' culture, the timing itself and a few other factors also contribute to the attribution of charisma to someone. Hence, we can only talk of charisma when there is empathy between leader and followers.

Like Kellett *et al* (2006) argue, empathy not only favours recognition of leadership, it also competes as a major mediating factor between the followers' emotions and those of the leader.

This empathetic relationship between Mourinho and his group is perceived by his own words, in his statement, during the Champions League final in Gelsenkirchen. The match was over, and so were the celebrations, and Mourinho waited for his players. He wrote: "*For the first time, I waited outside the dressing room and I kissed them all. May 26, 2004, Gelsenkirchen: we are immortal.*" (Mourinho *in* Lourenço 2004: 224)

Another example happened on his visit to Israel. In a speech before about 250 Israeli and Palestinian football coaches, Mourinho showed a photograph of himself embracing Chelsea player Frank Lampard and said: "*It looks like a hug, but it's more than that... it's a hug that shows that we trust each other. Without a word, he is saying to me: 'Thank you.' It's a hug that we repeat with all players, because we're a family.*" (Mourinho *in* Barclay 2006: 52)

How do we fit Mourinho's style of leadership in light of those who defend the existence of charismatic leadership? We already know that charisma is something assigned by certain factors. Immediately, this raises the question: is the origin of charisma in the individual, in the followers, in the situation, or in everything combined?

Consider Klein and House (1995) and their metaphorical formula that explains the emergence of any charismatic leadership. According to these authors, there are three parts involved in this emergence: the spark (the leader to whom characteristics and charismatic behaviours are attributed), the inflammable matter (followers receptive to the charisma) and oxygen (the charismatic environment, characterized by a crisis environment that led to low motivation).

When José Mourinho (the spark) arrived at FC Porto, the team (inflammable matter) occupied a modest sixth place in the Portuguese league, had been dismissed from the Portuguese Cup and were virtually out of the Champions League. Apart from this, it would be their third consecutive year without winning the national championship. The environment was obviously chaotic, with both players and fans (inflammable matter) not believing, in need of a direction, of someone that made them believe in something (oxygen). Mourinho arrived at FC Porto and, faced with these three elements, – also, being part of them – he created the necessary "ignition" for the emergence of his charismatic leadership. He created a spark by saying: *"Next year, we'll be champions."* This sentence was premeditated, because *"the team was as good as dead at that point"* (Mourinho *in* Lourenço 2004: 99), and Mourinho *"wanted to be clear to everybody at FC Porto, from the first day, that he was there to win"* (Lourenço 2004: 99). He also sought to "motivate the hosts" (Lourenço 2004) with an overall message to both the inside (everybody in the club) and the outside (all of Porto's supporters and even opponents).

And they were so motivated that, later, FC Porto's president Pinto da Costa, asserted *"with his presentation statement to the players – 'Next year, we'll be champions!' – he submitted his best calling card and his most perfect portrait. Confidence, determination, willingness to pass his untamed will to win to his people, everything was synthesized in that sentence"* (Pinto da Costa *in* Lourenço 2004: 98). From then on, we can say that Mourinho conquered the "nation" of FC Porto, and his attitudes as a leader constantly fed the flame of his charismatic leadership. After this, he told Porto's fans that the tie with Panathinaikos, who had won the first match in Antas, was not finished. After that, on his return to the Stadium of Light as FC Porto's manager, he entered the pitch before all of his players, facing a monumental chorus of whistles and boos from Benfica's fans, as Mourinho himself described in his biography:

> *I clearly knew that the minute I entered the pitch, I would have a thunderous reception... a bad one, of course. So I made sure to enter before the team, alone. When I stepped onto the pitch at the Stadium of Light for the first time on March 4, 2003, the stadium was full. We were still about an hour and a half away from the start of the match. It was fantastic. I felt something beautiful. I had never been a top player to feel, for example, what Figo felt when he returned to Barcelona, so I had no idea what would feel like to have 80,000 people whistling and hooting at me. I believe that when we are mentally strong, people who seek to intimidate and disrupt you fail completely. Rather, they give you strength and encouragement to continue your journey. The chorus of boos and whistles that Benfica's fans greeted me with at the Stadium of Light, made me feel like the most important person in the world. At the same time, they spared the team by booing me, which was also important.* (MOURINHO IN LOURENÇO 2004: 149)

SOME CHARACTERISTICS OF THE CHARISMATIC LEADER

As with any of us, our attitudes are directly linked to our personality traits. I will now emphasize five personal characteristics (not depleting the phenomenon of charisma), which constitute, to me, an almost genetic form we can find in anyone we consider a charismatic leader. The charismatic leader carries out an ambitious vision and articulates it with clarity; he takes personal risks; he's sensitive to the environment; he has a talent for communication and, a charismatic leader tends to stand out in some non-standard behaviour.

Let us see how Mourinho stands as a charismatic leader before this proposed formulation. The charismatic leader carries a vision and articulates it explicitly in order to promise, in a clear and well-defined manner, a better future for the whole team. Mourinho has well defined goals, whose sole purpose is to ensure victories. However, let me emphasize the practicability of Mourinho's proposed goals, essentially for two reasons: first of all, this practicability is due to Mourinho's way of being, which depends on the overall coherence between what's said and done, between the different treatment of people, and between what we want and the kind of work we do to achieve it. In this regard, Rui Faria said: "*Coherence implies achievable targets. (...) How can you make others believe in something you don't believe in yourself?*" This consistency is based on the evidence of the facts – to this day, Mourinho has always won trophies in every team he led from the beginning to the end of the season. The promise of victory also carries the promise of a more competent, and better future in terms of the group and the individuals. That was what happened when Mourinho arrived at Benfica. About what he told the players in their first contact, Mourinho stated: "*I promised them two things: first, the guarantee of 'work quality'. So, they would improve individually and collectively. The other promise was 'frankness'*" (Mourinho *in* Lourenço 2004: 39)

Personal risk is another characteristic of the charismatic leader. Leaders take risks, and they are prepared for failure that can lead to self-sacrifice in the name of a vision. When he arrived at FC Porto in January 2002, Mourinho didn't like many of the habits engrained in the team. He felt he needed to change, because there were people among the squad unwilling to change (Lourenço 2004). The manager took risks and faced the players at the end of a match, in Belém, where his team was heavily defeated by Belenenses: "*I told them that if I had to make history in the club as the coach who failed to qualify for European competition after so many years, I would. However, either things would change quickly or I would use the juniors, if needed be*" (Mourinho *in* Lourenço 2004: 109). This quote reveals another aspect of José Mourinho's work and leadership: his technical competence, his ability to diagnose what's going on in a group, to extract consequences thereof, to assume them and act based on that.

Sensitivity to the environment is another characteristic of Mourinho as a charismatic leader. In Rui Faria's words: "*The team structure is important but so are all surrounding structures. And when I say other structures, I mean different departments – the medical department, the football department, the kitman, the scouts... These are all interacting structures and can't be seen as something isolated."* For this reason, Mourinho says: *"It's not just us [the football team]. It's also the boss, the investors, the fans and so on."*

This attentiveness to what is outside his team, to the environment that surrounds it, enables us to understand the reason why Mourinho offered Chelsea's trophy, won in the United States, to the Stamford Bridge's groundsman. It was the beginning of the 2004/05 season. José Mourinho had arrived at the English club about a month before. The club was in pre-season and the first 30 days were of hard work at Stamford Bridge, Chelsea's stadium. Early on, the Portuguese manager had noticed that the pitch was in magnificent condition. These conditions allowed him excellent training sessions, that led to his first win in a tournament held in the United States, where the big draw was AC Milan, recently crowned European Champion. The trophy was lifted on the pitch by captain John Terry, but its fate was already sealed. In recognition for the groundsman's work, for the training sessions he provided the team, and whom José Mourinho considered one of the contributors for the victory, the trophy went straight to his house, upon its arrival in London. That man, who nobody except Mourinho had remembered when Chelsea won the trophy, had his deserved fifteen minutes of fame over the following days. British newspapers wanted to know about the destination of the trophy. Never before had a groundsman given so many interviews, seen so many photographs of himself in the papers and, more importantly, felt his work so recognized.

And with a more comprehensive look concerning the context of us all, Mourinho is also dedicated to humanitarian causes. For example, in December 2006, he agreed to be the patron for a London institution to support children with cancer, the CLIC Sargent. Furthermore, humanitarian causes are a goal Mourinho insists on extending beyond his own career as a football coach: *"Within thirteen years, when I have finished my work in football, I can see myself one hundred percent involved in humanitarian operations. I have always thought about the problems in the Middle East and Africa, not solely about football."* (Mourinho *in* Barclay 2006: 200-1)

Another characteristic that fits charismatic leadership and, consequently, Mourinho's leadership, relates to talent for communication.
In this respect, Mourinho feels like a fish in water. I recall the "points"
he scored when he presented himself in Italy, speaking fluent Italian.
I remember situations such as in Barcelona; after he revealed which
team would make the line up, he went further than any other coach
and also enumerated Frank Rijkaard's line up.

Jorge Costa is also enlightening when it comes to the topic of José
Mourinho's effective way of communicating:

*He is direct and effective in the way he communicates, you can feel
the security in his speech, the safe way he talks. Many managers who
believe in their players and their work can say that they hope to win or
draw at this or at that stadium, but it's another thing to say: "Where
is it? What stadium? It doesn't matter, I'm going there to win!" In the
first case, this speech doesn't motivate the players at all, because they're
not committed. In the second case, when the coach sticks his neck out
and says he'll win because his players are the best, then the players are
automatically committed to their leader, who is risking his neck for
them and that serves as motivating factor. This way, the players start
believing and having no doubts that they are the best and that they'll
win no matter where they go.*

Finally and to eliminate any questions – if there are still any questions – here are Frank Lampard's words, (Chelsea's vice-captain) in his
biography, describing how he saw him get to England and start dealing with the English press: *"From the moment I saw [Mourinho] handle
the media on his first day at Chelsea I knew that there was something
which set him apart from everyone else."* (Lampard 2006: 313)

Finally, the charismatic leader is also characterized by some kind
of unconventional behaviour. Many times, he adopts unusual new
behaviours that don't fit the pre-established rules. Reminding ourselves
of the beginning of José Mourinho's career, we conclude that this was
how he marked his entry into football. Mourinho came in with a different speech and different methods than usual, which caused many

different reactions. Right from the start, some people loved him and some people hated him.

Let us recall the words of football coach Manuel José, when he learned that Mourinho would replace him at União de Leiria: *"If Mourinho thinks this is a jungle and he is Tarzan, he's very wrong."* (Lourenço 2004: 77)

This sentence was uttered in a context where Manuel José thought Mourinho should have told him personally – which is not the norm in football, at least in Portugal – that he would be his replacement. However, it does not fail to mirror a less favourable environment that was cemented regarding Mourinho. Manuel José was not the only one; coaches, anonymous people, journalists and commentators, many have harshly criticized the then young coach – many still do today. Arrogant, selfish and insensitive were just some of the words that many people used when referring to him. Mourinho was seen as a threat, as someone who was breaking with the traditional canons. Mourinho was aware of this. He was already aware of this fact when he left Barcelona, before he even started his career as a professional football manager:

> *I know I'm going into a fight, into a medium where maybe I won't feel very comfortable, because the mentality is slightly different. Besides, I also know that I don't belong to the clan, to those who call the shots.* (MOURINHO IN LOURENÇO 2004: 24)

Mourinho knew he would face the powers that be, he knew he was different, that he would be different, and had already decided that his path was set and he would not divert from it. That is why he triggered hatred, but also passion.

> *José Mourinho [is not only] a good coach in the traditional sense. He's more than that: he's a new coach for a new football!"* (Sérgio in Lourenço 2003: preface), and that is, in Amhurst's words (2005:75), *what truly scares (...) others". José Mourinho "dared to contradict principles which, for years, had been the doctrine of generations of ill prepared managers, the prisoners of unacceptable subservience to equally*

unprepared leaders (...)" (Fernando Guerra in "A Bola", March 2ⁿᵈ, 2004). Mourinho's way of acting, his polemical style "in language and in deeds, irreverent, challenging, stimulating, combative, emotional and cold, also intelligent in off the pitch strategies, edgy, sometimes even fierce in his aggressiveness – and damn!, the technical quality of this young coach is a very serious matter, perhaps never seen before, not in Portugal at least.

(SANTOS NEVES IN THE NEWSPAPER "A BOLA", OCTOBER 3ᴿᴰ, 2003)

Desmond Morris noted what many have noted enough times:

[We] hang on his every word. He says relevant things that make you think. He avoids clichés. He was not caught up in the slack of the mindset 'That's Football'. (MORRIS IN BARCLAY 2006: 188)

Why? Leadership is only effective if it involves discovery and prophecy, i.e., if it leads to novelty, and conveys improvement of the self

The words and ideas of journalists, writers, managers, and university professors, mirror the way José Mourinho is regarded by many: a new leader, a charismatic man who came to break with the tradition. But this break is deeper than a mere change of style or culture. As we argue in this investigation, it's about action in a specific activity, as well as their understanding in light of the perspective of complexity, breaking with a centuries-old tradition of what we all received as an inheritance, consciously or unconsciously.

This is what I have been advocating in this study, albeit often implicitly: José Mourinho is the first professional in the world to put into practice the perspective of complexity in professional football coaching. He may be one of the first to fully carry out, to the smallest details of everyday action, that same paradigmatic perspective to any specific field of human action.

One of the challenges that will be referred to next (obviously outside the scope and possibilities of this book) is to study and develop the full transferability of José Mourinho's work to the world of organizations in general. In the case of leadership, an important topic in the contemporary organizational world, I tried to take the first step with the studies I started a few years ago. This book goes a little further.

A charismatic leader becomes one, largely by the traits described above; however, once the status is attained, the leader must keep the flame burning. The emergence of leadership is one thing; its maintenance is something else. How many cases could we name of leaders who emerged naturally and effectively at a given time, just to disappear shortly after in the limbo of vulgarity, and ended up being despised by those who so shortly before had followed them with such dedicated and almost blind allegiance?

Shamir *et al* (1993) propose a path for the charismatic leader; one where the present should be about experimenting the possibility and feasibility of a better future. Mourinho has used this approach in the clubs where he has been promising titles and victories – and has been achieving them. The charismatic leader announces his prospects and ambitions of high performance as well as his belief that these goals will be achieved. As mentioned above, Mourinho promises qualitative changes in each of his followers' skills, making them believe that they are capable of winning, and even that they are the best in the world. This attitude unleashes new feelings; it enhances the players' self-esteem and self-confidence and the results are visible, as we have shown and will continue to mention through statements by players like Drogba, Lampard, Jorge Costa, Vítor Baía and others.

According to Shamir *et al* (1993), in the trajectory of the charismatic leader, his behaviour stands out, which should be an example to his followers. At the same time it presents them a new value system – which, in Mourinho, is also reflected in the persistent message that the work of a football group doesn't end when one leaves the training or the stadium – the leader is always present, always displaying the code of conduct that should guide everyone in all facets of their lives, whether professional or social.

Lastly, the charismatic leader tends to sacrifice himself for the sake of the group. Mourinho's entrance at the Stadium of Light ahead of his players, to save them from the boos of Benfica's fans, is the proof of this.

Charismatic leadership causes direct effects on the followers. A relationship of cause/effect is seen between charismatic leadership and high performance on the one hand, and satisfaction of followers on the other hand. The high performance of Mourinho's athletes is demonstrated through the successes he gets in his groups. Regarding the satisfaction of those who work with him, here are the words of Vítor Baía, FC Porto's goalkeeper, quoted by Miguel Sousa Tavares: *"He's the best coach I've ever had. With him there is no training for entertainment or useless running around the field. Everything is done with the next game in mind and we only train how to win."* (Baía quoted by Sousa Tavares *in* Lourenço 2004: preface) Baía said this at a time when Mourinho had suspended him... These are Pedro Mendes' words, former player for Mourinho at Porto, when he played in England: *"He's a coach with a fantastic training methodology. Many Chelsea players are completely fascinated with the kind of work Mourinho is developing."* (Mendes *in* Jornal de Notícias, February 26, 2005)

Didier Drogba seems to have remembered Pedro Mendes' statement when he spoke to me five years later.

He has a different philosophy. For example, regarding training in all the clubs where I have been, we ran a lot before starting training with the ball, during pre-season. It was a way to regain fitness. Nothing like that happened with him. Absolutely everything was done with the ball, always with the ball, even the physical work. And I remember thinking to myself: 'What's going on? This is different from everything I know and did until today, I'm not sure this is correct'. But after starting to work that way, we begin to like what we're doing, and after realizing what is being done we say: what he [Mourinho] told us is true after all, it's working and he knows what he's doing.

We can conclude that José Mourinho is a charismatic leader, or someone who enjoys a powerful charismatic effect over his followers in the full technical assertion of this classification.

Transformational Leadership

Finally, I shall refer to one of the latest developments of neo-charismatic theories: Transactional Leadership and Transformational Leadership, proposed by Bernard Bass in the 1980s. These two theories complement each other, since the leader can use them both. Robbins (2002) argues that transformational leadership is built "upon" the Transactional leadership. Bass details this idea by stating that, in periods of foundation or organizational change, transformational leadership is the most effective one; in periods of organizational stability or slow evolution of the institution the transactional leadership applies with greater efficacy. One way or another, the two can complement and complete each other, and the leader can make use of both styles of leadership.

Due to its essence of stability, Transactional Leadership tends to be used on a day-to-day basis. The leader focuses their action on the followers' clarification, on the requirements and task development, using rewards or punishments for their achievement. By applying this notion to José Mourinho's daily work, and combining it with his notion of a group, let us recall Frank Lampard's words: *"Mourinho gives you the option: you can take the right route or the wrong one – but if you take the wrong route, he will know about it and there will be repercussions."* (Lampard 2006: 317) Here are Rui Faria's words, addressing the same topic, but focusing on a complex perspective:

> *The sanction aims at the reorganization of the whole, not as a punishment itself. It doesn't matter which player we punish. It's part of a structure that needs stability, because the disruption ultimately comes from each person's individuality.*

We saw how Mourinho deals with the punishment. Now let's see how he deals with rewards. In the Champions League final *"the great Pedro Emanuel, my right-hand man, suitable for all service"* (Mourinho *in* Lourenço 2004: 177) –that's how Mourinho referred to Pedro Emanuel, Porto's player, in his biography, when he recounts the Champions League final in Gelsenkirshen – was on the bench, sitting next to José Mourinho. Pedro Emanuel, for whom Mourinho had great respect and admiration, yearned to participate in the final as any player would. However, captain Jorge Costa was "filling in" for him. Five minutes before the end of the match, FC Porto was winning against Monaco by 3-0, and victory was assured. Jorge Costa's biography reports how Mourinho dealt with the moral problem of putting Pedro Emanuel on the field:

> *[Mourinho called Jorge Costa] to the sideline and asked him if he agreed to let Pedro Emanuel go in. Not because he felt that the result was at risk, but as a matter of justice to one of the leaders of the dressing room. (...) With his five minutes on the pitch, Pedro Emanuel was guaranteed his match fee, only paid to those who played, even if just for a minute.* (SANTOS E CERQUEIRA 2005: 118)

The real reward that Mourinho wanted to give Pedro Emanuel was for him to be able to participate in that match, so he could say he was a European champion. This was much more important than the monetary reward mentioned in Jorge Costa's biography – although this has to be considered, obviously.

Mourinho's direct leadership is exerted on a medium-sized group of about 33 people. Mourinho is both a day-to-day manager and a leader with vision. As we have just seen, he's a transactional leader; but he is also a transformational leader, as we shall see. That's Robbins' idea (2002) when he states that Transformational Leadership is built upon Transactional Leadership.

In its essence, what characterizes Transformational Leadership is that it *transforms* the objectives; somehow, it makes the group members forget their personal goals and replace them with the objectives of the group.

I remember Deco's words when he talked about Mourinho's FC Porto.

> *We were a very strong, cohesive group. We weren't just good players either, there was a lot of human quality. We also wanted to win, we had a huge ambition to win. On a personal level this ambition was*

natural, but beyond that, Mourinho managed to create a group ambition, so we liked to train, to play, to be together, and we did it gladly.

Deco's idea shows in a few lines the essence of transformational leadership in a strong and instructive manner. Individual goals don't disappear, they merely become secondary to the overall objectives of the group.

However, before we proceed to a more detailed analysis of Mourinho's Transformational Leadership, we need to clarify something. Transformational Leadership is largely confused with Charismatic Leadership. Both have a direct and positive impact on the followers, prompting them to achieve extraordinary results. Both methods of leadership instil high levels of confidence and motivation. Both prove to sponsor a moral the followers should live by. Both also indicate self-sacrifice. In conclusion, both Transformational Leadership and Charismatic Leadership focus on the interests of the organization, prompting the subordinates to overcome their personal interests on behalf of the group's objective. What distinguishes them, then? For starters, the notion that Transformational Leadership is somehow associated with Transactional Leadership. The assumption that the leader focused on every day and not just a vision for the future, with a prospect of change, is closer to the followers and has a more intimate relationship with them; he's not supposed to achieve charismatic leadership in day-to-day routine. The second distinguishing feature of Transformational Leadership compared to the Charismatic Leadership is that the charismatic leader's behaviour causes the followers to follow him, and adopt his vision, but that's it. The Transformational leader, on the other hand, tries to develop his followers' leadership instincts, making them more autonomous than the charismatic leader does. Avolio and Bass' words are easy to understand:

The purely charismatic leader may want his followers to adopt the vision of charismatic world. The transformational leader tries to instil in his followers the ability to question not only established views but also those put forth by the leader himself.

(AVOLIO E BASS IN ROBBINS 2002: 319)

In my opinion, these differences are not enough to make charismatic leadership autonomous, because the same principle prevails in both: the rule of consciousness and obvious motivation of the leader. For academic purposes, I made a clear distinction between both types of leadership. However, from my perspective, there's no reason to speak about both leadership types separately, because what distinguishes them is not essential and what unites them is too strong to be separated. I think charisma is an attribute – assigned or not, that's another issue – a personality trait of the human person and must be framed as such. Once framed, it takes us, to a large extent, to a type of leadership in which it fits and gets completed: the Transformational Leadership.

Charisma also serves to demonstrate (in some cases) and facilitate (in others) the emergence of leadership. Charisma fades out, and even tends to disappear.

What remains beyond that, then? The leader's profile and his leadership style. In conclusion, I believe that charisma fits certain kinds of leadership, makes their emergence easy, promotes their onset, but it always takes more than charisma to maintain an active leadership. In many cases, charisma disappears but leadership doesn't. Therefore, *"given the weak explanatory value as an isolated factor, scholars of leadership incorporate it in a broader concept – Transformational Leadership"* (Nye Jr, 2009: 89). Me too. Hence *"charisma, in the sense of personal magnetism is only part of transformational leadership"* (Nye Jr, 2009:89-90). What can we say about Peter Drucker's radicalism when he writes on the topic?

> *Leadership is important, of course. But, unfortunately, it's a different thing than what is now advocated. It has little to do with 'leadership qualities' and even less with 'charisma'. (...) History knows no more charismatic leaders than Stalin, Hitler and Mao – the pseudo leaders who have caused the greatest evil and suffering to mankind ever recorded. But effective leadership does not depend on charisma. Dwight Eisenhower, George Marshall and Harry Truman were particularly effective leaders, but they had as much charisma as a 'dead fish'.* (DRUCKER, 2008: 291)

As we saw earlier, Mourinho gathers charismatic characteristics. We won't focus on the characteristics that are common to this and to Transformational Leadership that I already enumerated. I will only refer to the features that go beyond his charisma, basing them solely in Transformational Leadership. I won't lose sight that this type of leadership is based on Transactional Leadership; therefore, I'll be looking at this transactional / transformational theme in its entirety.

According to the study by Karl *et al* (2003), there are four principles adopted by transformational leaders that produce direct results in their subordinates (they are intrinsically related to charisma). The first two – inspirational motivation and idealized influence – are directly related to charismatic leadership, and they have been analyzed above, albeit with a different terminology. It can be concluded that those two aspects characterize José Mourinho's behaviour. I understand that the third feature – the individualized consideration – is only partially inserted in the principles of charismatic leadership; therefore, it is more closely related to Transformational Leadership, whose theory we'll apply to José Mourinho's leadership. The last characteristic of the transformational leader – intellectual stimulation – is out of the sphere of Charismatic Leadership, so we will also address it in the context of José Mourinho's leadership.

Individualized consideration seeks motivation, appreciation, education and transfer of power to subordinates. Only this last aspect deviates from the principles of Charismatic Leadership, so we'll just focus on that.

First, let us divide Mourinho's followers into two groups: the coaching staff that is both leader (of the players) and follower (of José Mourinho), and the players, who just follow. We could consider the team captains as leaders as well, but this is irrelevant to this analysis. In the players group, there is no default delegation of power. The power delegation of the team captain is not an option of the coach, but rather a rule of the game; therefore, it can't be considered part of any kind of leadership. The essence of the players' work doesn't justify the existence of delegated powers. The task of players operating in a game is not in any way related to the leadership of the organization, either in the organizational sense, or in the operational sense. However, as was mentioned before, they contribute to the composition of the whole, by giving opinions and conveying ideas that can be used without it being a delegation of authority.

We can say that Mourinho delegates powers to the group consisting of the coaching staff without losing sight of the whole situation. In the delegation of power to any part of the coaching staff, Mourinho's global leadership remains always clear without, however, being understood as intruding, police-like or castrating. There is no transfer in delegated leadership, only solidarity and complicity – the execution is a guideline that everyone agrees with and carries out.

This idea has to be assumed as we start with the premise advocated throughout this book, that the perspective of complexity forms the basis of Mourinho's work. How can we understand his complex work basis in a leadership centred on José Mourinho? As follows: Mourinho has the *dominant* leadership of his group; however, in a given context, any adjunct can assume a clear leadership role. This idea is implied in Mourinho's words:

Rui [Faria] is my complement. In fact, I don't even call him fitness coach, because he's much more than that and this concept doesn't exist in our working model; in reality, he performs and coordinates a large part of our training methodology.

(MOURINHO IN OLIVEIRA ET AL 2006: 45-6)

By leaving to Rui Faria part of the execution and coordination of the work of the command team, Mourinho is delegating powers, not centralizing powers. This happens with Rui Faria and with the remaining coaching staff, because it would make no sense in a complex perspective that Mourinho – with or without Rui Faria – was a separate part of the whole, a different and distinctive element – in its organic and in the its operability – of a whole composed of parts that make up and constantly reshape that same whole.

Finally, the characteristic of intellectual stimulation is intended to get the subordinates to question themselves and the *status quo*. It also seeks to encourage innovation and creativity to a joint resolution of the problems of the organization. In this area, it should be noted that

Mourinho, on principle, wants smart players in his teams that, some-how, hints at the importance that the ability of individual reflection assumes. It would be a contradiction that Mourinho gave relevance to his follower's intelligence and then would not use it. Rui Faria empha-sizes: *"From a mental point of view aimed at the game, since what you do is to acquire mental and behavioural training, the players have to think and be smart to observe. That's why José Mourinho says he just wants smart players in his teams."*

However, it is also true that you can't just be smart in what the leader wants and stop being smart in any unpredictable situation you find yourself in. Therefore, the intelligence desired by Mourinho can only be understood in the overall work and on the whole of what he expects, in the game and out of it, from each of his followers. That's how Mourinho introduces his followers to *Guided Discovery*, a method which (as we have seen) seeks that the players discover their own path under the guidance and the clues given by the leader.

The path, therefore – as Miguel Unamuno (1864-1931) wrote – is made as you go, as you feel, learn and seize, each one thinking and feeling in a complex perspective.

Mourinho accepts the questioning and the brainstorming by his followers without deviating, at least in a substantial way, from the route he has already mapped out. That's why he needs the individ-ual intelligence at the service of questioning and doubting. It is also through *Guided Discovery* that Mourinho encourages individual inno-vation and creativity at the service of problem solving for the group and for the organization as a whole.

4. EMOTIONAL INTELLIGENCE

In the current globalization we must live conscious of the fact that we can work anywhere in the world at any time. In such circumstances, our academic skills have little importance, and we often prove that our emotions win over professional talent when we are betrayed by the longing or anxiety about the things we leave behind. (SOTO, 2001: 4)

How can we subtract emotions from human thought turned into action, given that, in a complex perspective – and even in the exact sciences, as Damásio will prove to us – they remain with us throughout our existence, and are part of the complex whole that is us?

The issue of the emotional weight in our "internal theatre" results from a simple question: what weight do our emotions have when we talk about leadership, decision-making, and the attitude towards self and others? Until recently it was thought that it had none. Leaders and managers around the world, coming from a Cartesian mechanistic point of view, with its resulting division, separation and loss of context of the object of study, understood that the decision process was made based on a single element: reason. Extending this concept to the subject of leadership, we can imagine the idea of leader – and leadership – underlying it with relative ease. It's the straightforward frontal man who decides with a clear head, with rigor, without doubts or emotions. The aim was to convey the leader's security on his competence and his decisions before everything else. The detached leader, as if out of the world of uncertainty, ambiguity and emotions, was at the highest level of the organization, therefore exerting his authority in a distant and safe way. Being emotional or showing feelings was synonymous with weakness, which was not accepted then as still tends to not be accepted today. But things are changing.

DAMÁSIO'S STUDIES

António Damásio, the Portuguese neuroscientist, who has lived in the U.S. for over 30 years, currently a professor and director of the Department of Neurology at the University of Iowa – defined emotion as: *"Basically, emotions enable an automatic reaction to a series of threats or opportunities faced by a living organism."* (Damásio *in* Marques 2004:68) If emotions make us react automatically, we can presume this reaction doesn't depend on us as the only option of reason, and it will be fair to say we're doomed to work with them in all the active processes of our lives. As we can't help but thinking, we can't also think without emotions, unless we are biologically prevented to do so. But if that happened, would we still be ourselves? Would we continue to look at the world in the same way? Could our actions still be predictable given our history?

Starting from the scientific fact that our emotional system is located and perfectly defined in a part of our brain, Damásio (2005) tells a story based on his research, which suggests answers to the questions above.

Elliot[17], a North-American citizen in his thirties, lived a successful life. A beloved husband and father, a recognized expert, he led the quiet life of a successful man both professionally and socially, until the day he was diagnosed with a brain tumour. It wasn't malignant and its extraction would solve the problem, because once removed, the doctors were convinced that it wouldn't grow back. The surgery was an apparent success and the outlook was excellent. The tumour was removed, as well as the damaged *frontal lobe* tissue. According to what Damásio (2005) describes, many and new problems were yet to come. During recovery, family and friends began to notice significant differences in Elliot's behaviour. A new Elliot now revealed himself in contrast to the active, stable and balanced man. He needed incentives to go to work, very rarely finished a task, and instability became part of his life to the point that Elliot became unable to make decisions.

---

[17] Fictitious name given by Damásio, because the real person is under medical confidentiality.

His new personality quickly led to two divorces and multiple layoffs in the various jobs he got later. Clearly, *"Elliot was no longer Elliot"* (Damásio 2005:56) and his life became chaotic. Elliot kept all his mental and physical abilities intact, despite the fact that all of his personality traits were different now. Elliot's reasoning was not disturbed, his IQ remained above average, as it was confirmed by tests, and his senses were all unchanged. Thus, to some extent, Elliot was still Elliot. He remained the same as far as his neurological abilities, but he was different regarding the operation of those same abilities.

His problems were not the result of 'organic disease' or 'neurological dysfunction' – a brain disease – but rather the reflection of 'emotional' and 'psychological' adjustment problems. (DAMÁSIO 2005: 59-60)

Elliot was a man with a perfectly normal intellect who betrayed himself by his inability to make decisions, especially when they were of a personal or social nature. As Damásio's patient, Elliot performed all kinds of tests, until the doctor began to divert his attention to an issue that was almost ignored: the emotions. After another of the numerous sessions with Elliot, Damásio (2005) was able to confirm that this could be the path to find out what was happening. He showed his patient pictures of disasters such as burning houses, of buildings collapsing in earthquakes, of wounded people, etc., trying to understand how he reacted to emotionally strong and disconcerting stimuli.

He told me, unequivocally, that his feelings had changed since his illness. He realized that the topics that had previously raised strong emotions in him no longer caused any reaction, positive or negative.

(DAMÁSIO 2005: 64-65)

At this point, light began to shine in Damásio's investigation. Imagine that, while watching a Chelsea football match, José Mourinho's most fanatical fan suddenly realized that it meant nothing to him anymore. Imagine a goal in the Champions League final and a fan's emotional reaction being like drinking a glass of water. Or, imagine someone contemplating a magnificent landscape and experiencing a feeling of triviality. In both cases, people had already experienced strong, sweeping feelings in similar situations, and now they realized what was wrong, i.e., they had already felt emotions in similar situations and were now fully aware they felt nothing. There could be many more examples, but these are sufficient to realize Elliot's state: knowing but not feeling (Damásio 2005). In other words, Elliot was aware of everything in the world around him, he knew the difference between good and evil, right and wrong, white and black, but he could not give them a function in real life. Being deprived of emotions, it was irrelevant for him to follow one path rather than another. He could not make decisions; he was not able to make choices. Damásio writes that he started *"thinking that the coldness of Elliot's reasoning prevented him from assigning different 'values' to different options, making his landscape in decision-making hopelessly flat."* (Damásio 2005: 70)

After Elliot and until 1993, Damásio studied 12 other similar cases of prefrontal lesions. The scientist noticed links between loss of emotions and disability in decision-making in all of them. Damásio explains the reasons for this association in his works *O Erro de Descartes* (1995), *O Sentimento de Si* (2000) and *Ao Encontro de Espinosa* (2003).

GOLEMAN'S THEORY – EMOTIONAL INTELLIGENCE

With this example, I want to illustrate the connection between emotions and the leader's behaviour. The emotions are closely linked to the leader, so that the behavioural construction will never be the same. If he's seriously conditioned by emotions, he'll lose his functionality, either by their absence, or by *excess*.

We all know that excessive emotions bring behavioural changes. Just think about some of our attitudes when we experience high levels of anxiety or nervousness. What we did not yet know – and Damásio's work (1995, 2000, 2003) proved, – is that their absence could lead to a completely flat landscape of decision; that without emotions we cannot make decisions.

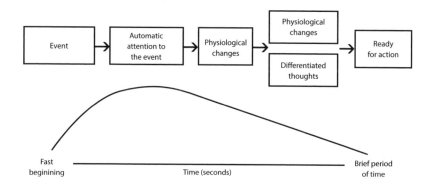

So when we think we have to make a decision without any emotional influence, we are making a mistake because emotions are always there with us, sometimes imperceptible, but always there, active, and an integral part of our decision-making process. It is pertinent to raise some questions: if emotions are an integral part of our life; if their absence or excess fundamentally changes our behaviour; if we're condemned to live with them (for better or worse) is it rational for us to let them evolve or change, acting without any control or influence over them? Is it reasonable to not look at emotions, not ask how, and in what way they can be more useful, how we can optimize them in our actions? Isn't it better to know them for their most effective use and to what extent they can and/or should be used? And if emotions constitute a key factor of influence on our character and behaviour, won't a more effective control over them be relevant, based on this knowledge? The theory of Emotional Intelligence tells us so. It goes even further: not only does it tell us yes, it also points out the paths. It gives us clues to be intelligent about our emotions and the emotions of others, so that we can benefit from them and avoid their adverse effects against the threats and opportunities that we face in our everyday lives.

What are emotions for, objectively? In his book *The Expression of Emotions on Man and Animals* published in 1872 – translated into Portuguese (Darwin 2006) – Charles Darwin (1809-1882) explains how emotions are a complex but effective system of adapting to the surroundings. After we get burned, we begin to have an emotional relationship with fire, which protects us from getting burnt more often. A car that appears at high speed scaring us when we cross the street, makes us pay more attention the next time, giving us the strength and speed that allow us to run to safety.

Etymologically speaking, emotion is *attention, to move towards*. The act or action is implicit in emotions, as indeed, it could have been already concluded from the definition presented by Damásio (2005). In a more productive plan than that transcribed above, Damásio concludes on what he considers emotion to be:

Emotion is the combination of a mental evaluative process, which can be simple or complex, with dispositional responses to that process. These are mostly directed at the body itself, resulting in an emotional state of the body, but also directed at the brain (neurotransmitters in the brain stem nuclei), resulting in additional mental changes.

(DAMÁSIO 2005: 153)

Thus, an emotion is seen as a response to an external element; in other words, as a reactive state of mind in which reason is not called upon to participate. So, if the reaction is transformed into action, we'll just react on impulse. If we don't have action coordinated (weighted, balanced) with emotion and reason, it will certainly enhance the probability of error in the answer.

Goleman *et al* (1995: 310) also defined emotion by referring to a *"feeling and reasoning derived from it, psychological and biological states, and the range of propensity for action"*. I think the differences between this notion and Damásio's notion (2005) is that they are more concerned with the object of study of each of them rather than structural differences. A combination between both definitions can be made, so that you can work them together without conflicts in the goals we wish to explore.

We conclude that Goleman *et al* as well as Damásio talk about emotional states arising from (mainly) external factors that predispose us to action and reaction. Therefore, in a logical sequence of ideas, it can be concluded that emotions are nothing more than mechanisms to help us:

– to react quickly against unexpected events;
– to make decisions promptly and safely, and
– to communicate nonverbally with other people.

(MÄRTIN, BOECK 2007 : 32)

It is now explicit what emotions are and we also know they are always present throughout our lives. We also know that they can be used for excess, which consequently, can lead to making bad decisions – precisely what we want to avoid in every conscious act of our lives. What we do not yet know is how we can use them in the exact extent to improve our behaviour.

In the 1996 book, as well as in the 1998 article "What Makes a Leader", published in the *Harvard Business Review*, Goleman *et al* (2005) and Goleman (1998) pointed the intelligence quotient and the technical qualifications of leaders as the most important characteristics of leadership. Their investigations indicated that, despite the degree of importance of analytical intelligence and mathematics, Emotional Intelligence could be the *sine qua non* condition for a good leadership.

But what is Emotional Intelligence, after all? In a simplistic way, we can say that we are being emotionally intelligent when we can be intelligent about our emotions. In Emotional Intelligence, it is assumed that we can consciously deal with our emotions and others', give them direction and leverage them effectively, not in an isolated form, but rather combined with reason. The absence of this combi-nation – devoid of emotion (*one of the structural elements*) made Elliot (*who knows but does not feel*) different from most humans (who know and feel). So, Goleman (1995) proposed the theory of *two minds*, whereby we have precisely two minds: one that thinks (and deals with reason) and another that feels (and deals with emotion). Strictly speaking, there are two different ways of knowing, of understanding our own way of being, but which are always present in us, interacting. This way, becoming our way of being *in two minds*, we can't wilfully not think and not have emotions. These *two minds* tend to work in balance to guide us in our actions.

Under normal conditions, the emotional and rational brain regions work as a team that works in harmonic form: emotions are important for thinking, thoughts are important for the emotions.

(MÄRTIN, BOECK 2997: 31)

The *two minds* are formed in an open system and therefore are subject to outside pressures. The threats and opportunities in the environment lead them towards balance even though they may experience chaotic situations. These occur when there is an imbalance, when one part tends to excel over the other. For example:

A simple word of an inadequate interlocutor, a melody that reminds us of a past and finished relationship, the odour of a sunscreen, or a sweet look can trigger feelings of anger, tenderness or nostalgia.

(MÄRTIN, BOECK 1997: 31)

When reason ignores emotion or when emotion takes charge of reason, the scale is unbalanced. One mind takes over another, one loses the ability to intervene and, by doing so, the probability of error in our performance increases exponentially. Feelings, rather than thoughts are the decisive factor for Man. That's why, at this point, we leave the "I think, therefore I am" to enter the field of "I feel, therefore I am."

The theory of two minds – acting in a complex system of thinking in constant interaction, making it impossible to separate or take them out of context, because "Elliot stops being Elliot" – requires the right balance between the two, a stable state of the human being. From there, it's possible "to play" with our emotions and use them to our advantage, so we can become emotionally intelligent.

I can't stress enough what I have said previously. It's true that the theory of Emotional Intelligence can be applied to any act or circumstance of our lives; however, the object of this work focuses on leadership and the process of communication and interaction in which it is reflected.

I remember going to Stamford Bridge in March 2005, to watch the Champions League match between José Mourinho's team and Seville.

In the middle of the second half, Chelsea was winning 4-0, making the English supporters who completely filled the stadium rave. Suddenly, all the spectators started a song with a single sentence, in unison: *"Stand up, stand up for the Special One."* At the same time, the entire stadium stood up while they were singing, and they bowed towards José Mourinho, who was still sitting on the bench. I remained seated, just like José Mourinho, looking around and contemplating the spectacle provided by Chelsea's supporters. However, I didn't remain seated for long… Suddenly, one of them looked a bit angrily at me and, while intoning the chants directed at Mourinho, signalled me with both hands so that I, too, got up and took a due bow to their leader, the "Special One". So, that's what I did.

This example is to say: *"Great leaders move us. They ignite our passion and inspire the best within us. (…) Great Leadership is based on emotions"* (Goleman *et al* 2003), not in a purely / solely transitive and manipulative way, but from the basis of all creative emotion – in this case, the leader's heart. What raises emotion in us, followers, is the emotion that someone causes. The feelings that leaders create in their followers can cause them to better themselves and get unexpected results, simply because people trust their leader and believe that, under his leadership, they will achieve better results. So they follow him over and over, almost blindly.

Let us recall the defeat of FC Porto at home with the Greeks of Panathinaikos. At the end of the match where FC Porto lost 1-0, as you recall, Mourinho said to FC Porto's fans and his players that it wasn't finished yet and that they would win the next round and go to the semi-finals in Greece. FC Porto's fans believed it would be so, and when they saw Mourinho in the street, they reminded him: *"We're going there to win because you promised."* Players also believed in their leader's promise and they won the second match 2-0 and went through to the semi-finals. This episode illustrates the importance of communication that leads to empathy and charisma between leader and followers. The impact of the message over the people's state of mind is paramount; therefore the role of emotions in followers – because there are no leaders without followers – is often the difference between being or not being… a leader.

This is how Vítor Baía recalls the importance of emotion in Mourinho as a powerful weapon to condition and influence the world around him:

> *He gets the best out of his players through his leadership, and that makes all the difference. In addition, he's also able to have control over very important areas such as human resources. He handles the psychological and emotional part of people very well, and he pioneered the use of psychology and brought it to sport. It's the combination of both that builds his efficacy. Obviously, he is also a born strategist who works for both the outside and inside of his teams. When he works to the outside, he always has an effective strategy: to place a large emotional charge in everything, protect and take pressure off everything that belongs to the team and is behind him, and cause the other (the opponent, the opposing coach, the media, etc.) various well-defined gaps that he tries to accomplish. At the same time, these attitudes always have an action for the interior, because in this 'war' we must also protect him, that is, we have to go down to the 'death' with him and he prepares us for that as well. In FC Porto, he had the added convenience of a team that was already special – we already have this culture in FC Porto, we're warriors by nature, we're people who don't care to 'die' on the pitch, who are supportive and this is the culture of the club. He helped us to put into practice all that we had inside in a natural way. He taught us how to better carry out that culture of club, so that we could improve our skills, our confidence and our game. So this was one of his strengths.*

In developing their ideas, Goleman, Richard Boyatzis and Annie McKee (2003) show us in their book, *Os Novos Líderes – A Inteligência Emocional nas Organizações*, a new concept: *primal leadership.* Goleman *et al* argue that *"the emotional role of the leader is primal – that is, it comes first – in two ways. It is the first act of leadership and, at the same time, the most important one."* (Goleman *et al* 2003: 25) One of the leader's main actions involves leading the collective emotions of his followers in order to achieve superior results and effects from the mere positive performance of tasks.

This aspect, as we shall see, is fundamentally important – together with others, as conditioning the opponents' attitudes and decisions – in José Mourinho's leadership. Here too, the "whole" is different and more valuable than the sum of its parts. Beyond just technical leadership – the leader knows more, has greater knowledge about the subject matter – followers seek a *"relationship of emotional support"* (Goleman *et al* 2003), an empathic communication. Therefore, leadership always intersects with this *primal* dimension, as Goleman *et al* argue. The emotional role of the leader is the first and most important act of leadership; because people, especially in a time of crisis, always need and seek emotional orientation.

This dimension fits and works in the whole that is the leader's Emotional Intelligence. This is his virtue; the way he knows, understands and manages his emotions and those of others. We are talking about an open system as opposed to closed systems. In the latter, there is no communication or interactive dynamics.

To clarify, let's look at the example of the human being's circulatory system (Goleman *et al* 2003). What is happening in my system does not affect what is happening in my neighbour's. Indeed, this is not what happens when emotions are involved. In this case, we talk about an open system because emotions interact amongst different individuals. My joy or my sadness cause – or can cause – similar states or changes of emotional state to those who deal with me on a daily basis. The same principle applies to the leader and leadership in the relationship he has with his followers, hence, we should talk about contagion. Then, we can understand the criticism that Mourinho was subjected to by his followers for not celebrating the victory in the Champions League with them; while the entourage arrived at Oporto and paraded through the streets, their leader took refuge at home away from the festival and the crowds (Lourenço 2004)[18]. For better or for worse, everyone looks at the leader, the spotlight is always on him and he contaminates not only by what he says but also by the emotions he causes, which go far beyond his words. Whatever the situation

---

[18] In a bizarre but real episode, José Mourinho was under death threats, as the press reported at the time and Lourenço (2004) mentions.

is, it's up to the leader to make the people he works with be the best they can be, to make them more valid, more competent and happier. When he can do it, Goleman *et al* (2003) say that the leader creates *resonance*. When the opposite happens, the leader creates *dissonance*.

Leadership is required to create resonance and there are many ways to convey feelings that may or may not create resonance. So, we can understand the resonance that Mourinho created in Chelsea's fans who stood up while singing in unison and took a bow to the "Special One". The resonance Mourinho created, with a simple gesture, between FC Porto's fans and staff promising them victory in Greece after the match with Panathinaikos, is understandable. Many other examples could be given here about leadership with resonance that José Mourinho creates in his followers or opponents. And since no examples were given from the opponents' perspective, I think it's relevant to recount Mourinho's own words when I asked him about the nickname that the British media gave him in this regard: the "Master of the Mind Games".

I don't know whether or not I am the 'Master of the Mind Games' as they used to say in England. What I do know is that the mind games don't affect me and, because of that, I feel comfortable looking for others' weaknesses if there are any. So, as far as I am concerned, they can say whatever they want about me, my team or my players; for me, there's no difference. There's not a single comment, or a statement from a coach, a statement from an opposing player that can affect me in any way or change my way of thinking regarding anything. Quite the contrary, I have clearly felt that my statements have modified behaviours throughout my career. Obviously, I don't mean that everyone does, nor all the time, but it happens often, and so I think that's a path to explore and that's what I have been doing.

It is clear that, in Mourinho, his immunity to others' mind games constitutes the secret of his leadership: his power comes from within. He shapes the circumstances, not the other way around.

Hence, the visible and extraordinary effects he also triggers in his players, as Jorge Costa told me:

First: in so doing, he freed us from a great many things. I'm talking about pressure, stress, etc., because that's what happens when we play in big teams, as was the case of FC Porto. Therefore, the fact that he engaged himself in all these wars meant that we were apart, removed from the superfluous and concentrated on the essential – the training sessions and the match.

Second: since he engaged in the wars, we were 'forced' to be the warriors to back him up. So, as his warriors, our response to those wars was to beat the opponent on the pitch. We felt it had to be this way, it was a commitment. It seems easy, but it isn't. In order to achieve this, you must create a good group, united and willing to do anything, and as I said, this isn't easy; even Mourinho himself can eventually find a group in which he won't be able to get all that complicity.

Areas of Emotional Intelligence

In what ways can a leader reach this state of grace to lead with emotional resonance or to have an effective leadership? Goleman *et al* (2003) tell us about *areas* of Emotional Intelligence and name four[19]: self-awareness, self-management, social awareness and relationship management. Let's say this is the ground the emotional leader will have to inhabit. Half of the ground (the first two) consists of *personal skills* and determines the person's self-management. The other half is made up of the *social skills* that determine the management of relations between my emotional self and others. All these areas are interconnected and interact with each other through their various associated skills, of which there are eighteen. In this analysis, I won't review each of these skills in detail. I don't need details to characterize José Mourinho's leadership. Therefore, I will only list the areas listed above.

Self-consciousness, whose associated skills are emotional self-awareness, self-evaluation and self-confidence, is defined by the ability we have to know ourselves as beings with qualities, flaws, limitations,

---

[19] In the beginning of his studies, Goleman pointed to five areas of EI: Self-Awareness, Self-Management, Motivation, Empathy and Social Aptitude.

ambitions, motivations and values. Only by knowing our emotions and ourselves may we be able to know others and their emotions. Self-consciousness can be considered as the basis of Emotional Intelligence.

Self-management includes the competencies of emotional self-control, transparency, adaptability, ability to perform, capacity for initiative and optimism and is a part of self-awareness (Goleman *et al* 2003). It is based on energy that leaders need to achieve their goals. The leader must control his emotions – in this case, negative or disturbing emotions that produce negative feelings as opposed to positive ones, which are the best in us – so he's not their hostage. Thus, we can understand that the leaders' state of mind does not only belong to the sphere of their personal behaviour. As mentioned above, due to the leader's emotional contagion, his emotions have consequences for his team and for the public. Therefore, *"no leader is able to manage other people's emotions if he's unable to manage his own"* (Goleman *et al* 2003: 66).

Social consciousness includes skills such as the spirit of service, organizational awareness and empathy, the latter being clearly the most important one. This is the key area to generate resonance, which is why empathy is so important. If he is in tune with the followers, the leader can decide on the best way to make the most of his emotions and those of others. He can contain tensions or share happiness, appease optimism or relieve pessimism; he can and should generate the balance that serves the tasks.

Finally, relationship management encompasses inspirational leadership, influence, ability to develop others, catalyze change, conflict management, the establishment of ties and team spirit and collaboration. Relationship management begins with authenticity – being honest, doing what you say and saying what you do – a key feature for relationships with others. A true leader inspires trust and this facilitates the ability of persuasion, of conflict management, of willingness to change and of cooperation of followers. Thus, enthusiasm around a common project becomes easier and more effective.

EMOTIONAL LEADERSHIP STYLES

Effective Emotional Intelligence involves those areas because the majority of its skills should and must be used. However, it is the character – the set of unique individual features – of each of us that enables this whole to be used, acting in different dosages. It is this dosage, namely, the leader's ability to use or rely more on this or that aspect, to a greater or lesser degree, on this or that circumstance, that produces the different leadership styles.

Goleman *et al* (2003) propose us six leadership styles; however, each leader can match more than one leadership style. A leader can be seduced by a style in a striking manner, but nothing prevents him from acting more in line with another style that can produce more effective results.

This aspect helps us realize another type of division. Out of the six styles, four of them – visionary, counsellor, relational and democratic – generate resonance. The other two – authoritarian and commanding, tend to produce dissonance, except in very specific situations.

VISIONARY STYLE   Perhaps the most important feature of the visionary leader is to inspire his followers. However, the secret is in how he does it. This leadership type is supported by how it expresses its objectives. He demands from others what he demands from himself. This leader is in tune with his subordinates because he shares the same values, so he's authentic. He doesn't instil ideas and purposes in them, he let's them discover it for themselves, and genuinely believes in them, although conditioned by the way the leader proposes them and the goals to be achieved. The visionary leader leads his followers to fulfil their tasks in an engaging manner; he leaves space for them to find a way that he himself has imagined. For Mourinho, that's what the technique nicknamed *Guided Discovery* does. His authenticity and the shared values he preaches are well expressed when, after the defeat with Panathinaikos, he told his players: *"We'll turn this around, and if anyone here doesn't believe that it is possible to win there and move on to the semi-finals, tell me now, because you'll stay here and I'll go to Greece with someone else."* (Lourenço 2004: 151)

ADVISOR STYLE This style finds much of its foundation in the leader's relational capacity with each of his subordinates. The leader sees the man beyond the professional and is interested in his well being, in and out of work. He talks, listens and advises on an individual basis, because every human being is different and unique. Goleman believes that this style is not very practiced nowadays being, however, capable of generating resonance, since the advisor leaders (by establishing connections) help people identify their strengths and weaknesses, creating a direct link to their actual performance. Maybe this is not his strong point, but José Mourinho can also find some grounds for his leadership here. We can see this in Desmond Morris'[20] words: *"Mourinho identifies himself with his team more than any other coach. He is passionately involved with them. (...) I slightly disagree from those who see him like a father to his players. He is more like an older brother. Or the ringleader."* (Morris *in* Barclay 2006: 157-8)

RELATIONAL STYLE This style is characterized by shared emotions. The leader celebrates and mourns. He places the emphasis on the human being and his feelings more than on the professional and, in doing so, he creates great bonds of loyalty and relationship. It is, however, a leadership style that doesn't improve people's performances directly. Although Mourinho gets emotional with his players, we can't consider him a relational leader, since he rarely admits mistakes and is always looking for the individual and collective perfecting in a direct way, which is the most important thing for him. In a complex perspective, he doesn't dissociate personal happiness from personal performance, as can be seen from the words of Chelsea player Joe Cole: *"He is the first person to seriously look at me and my way of playing."* (Cole *in* Barclay 2006: 142)

DEMOCRATIC STYLE The democratic leader, as the name implies, uses personal contacts, discussion, sharing of ideas and suggestions. He does so in meetings, which can be extended, and he listens to the participants' concerns. By listening to others, he finds much of the foundation for his own decision making process. He

---

[20] Author of the celebrated bestseller The Naked Ape.

creates an overall positive emotional climate and works better if the leader has doubts. José Mourinho's own personality, technical knowledge and competence don't fit him directly in this style of leadership, as the final analysis will attest.

The four styles of leadership I have just mentioned generate resonance, to a greater or lesser degree. Now, let's see a brief description of two styles that should be used very carefully or its final outcome may be disastrous, because it generates dissonance.

COMMANDING STYLE   It is a style of conduct used in certain contexts because it does not draw clear lines of action. Most of the time, the leader is focused on the objectives, instead of on his followers, which could result – and in the medium/long run surely does – in dissonance. However, as mentioned before, in a given context and in moderate doses, pressure can lead to positive performances. It's a style that José Mourinho may or may not identify himself with. Let's remember his entrance before his players at the Stadium of Light for the Benfica v FC Porto match in 2003, as a way to relieve the pressure exerted by Benfica's fans. Mourinho always tries to take the pressure off – either excess or inappropriate pressure – from those who work with him. However, in this example the pressure comes from outside the team, not from the leader. When we talk about pressure from the leader – and here the framework of the commanding style shall be correct – we can say that José Mourinho also fits this style of leadership. Here are Rui Faria's words to prove this analysis: *"Those who live with him professionally have to learn to live under great pressure and at the same time must respond positively. The pressure that José Mourinho puts on his workgroup is done in a very particular way according to different situations."* Mourinho pushes the players, challenging them constantly and consistently, to do their utmost, to excel, and to be the best.

AUTHORITARIAN STYLE   This style of leadership calls for blind obedience, which connects it to a highly coercive way of being. In today's society it is the least acceptable and tolerable; it may nevertheless be accepted in very occasional situations, such as threats, for example.

Before we end this chapter, I cannot resist transcribing Deco's words that fit and illustrate almost perfectly all that was said above about Mourinho's Emotional Intelligence. It is Deco's vision of Mourinho's emotional acting illustrated with a delightful story. It's worth reading carefully and smiling at the end.

I have had other managers that, for example, regarding motivation were and are very good, but Mourinho achieved some things that others didn't. In a very short time, he was able to know all individual players and their personality. In a group, one must have the perception of the group, know how the group functions as a whole to be able to motivate and have that natural perception of the individual separately, know how he works in order to motivate him on an individual level. In short, to know how the player reacts when faced with situations and act accordingly, and get the best that the player has to give. This is about making a psychological management of the player.

Do you have any example of this psychological management?

Yes, I can give you an example of a player who was very peculiar: Maniche. Before an important match, like a game in the Champions League, one that Mourinho knew he needed him in, because he was a fantastic player, the best in FC Porto, and one or two matches before the big one, Mourinho took him out of the team and sat him on the bench. Maniche was a very explosive player and he "saw red" at being made to go on the bench; he grumbled, cursing life and the coach, etc. I understood everything but said nothing. I understood what Mourinho wanted to provoke in Maniche, and the truth is it always got the desired effect. Maniche saw red, and at the time he returned, angry at the situation, he always played with the idea of playing the best game of his life. And Maniche never realized that that was what Mourinho wanted. In fact, he couldn't know, otherwise the intended effect would be lost.

In England, Mourinho was known as the "Master of the Mind Games". Can you say that he "played" with your emotions?

Yes, you can. He had a perception of how each of us worked and used it for the sake of the group. Sometimes, he even caused stressful situations in a certain match, but always with some purpose.

The theory of Emotional Intelligence that, from the perspective of complexity, is one of the theoretical bases of all the work done by José Mourinho, is thus revised. I have shown that its main concept – emotion – is something intrinsic to our nature. Emotional Intelligence tells us that we must be smart about our emotions and those of others, a notion that is applied with greater intensity to the leaders.

5. CONTEXTUAL INTELLIGENCE

No generalization is wholly true – not even this one.
(OLIVER WENDELL HOLMES IN KELLY, 2009:17)

It is not enough to conquer wisdom, it is necessary to use it.
(CICERO – PHILOSOPHER 106 BC - 43 BC)

The concept has been developed by many scholars, in such a way that it has even gone into other fields of intelligence. This is how we find the concept of Contextual Intelligence, which I believe fits in Mourinho's way of being, living and leading.

As I said, we live in an era of change, which forces us and requires the leader to constantly adjust to reality. Different realities change markets and the visions and strategies are also subject to frequent changes. It's about creating intelligent strategies according to each situation; aligning them with the constantly renewed future that causes change or turbulence every day. In short, to level the sight as the target moves.

This idea is only achievable if you diagnose and understand the context in which we are integrated. So Anthony Mayo and Nithin Nohria of Harvard Business School, cited by Nye Jr. (2009: 121-122), defined Contextual intelligence as *"the ability to understand a changing environment and to take advantage of trends."*

These researchers tried to explain the reasons why certain companies are able to adapt to new markets and others aren't, concluding that this ability is based on the leader's intuition to anticipate new tactics for new purposes in times of change. This intuition justifies the emergence of this concept; otherwise we would have the contingency theories to explain and justify context-based leadership.

According to Nye Jr.:

Contextual intelligence involves the capacity to discern trends in complex contexts and adaptability to them. (...) Leaders with Contextual intelligence have the ability to provide a direction or guideline by defining the problem the group faces. (...) Contextual Intelligence involves the use of the flow of events to implement a strategy. It allows leaders to adjust their style to each situation and the particular needs of their followers, and create information flows that can complement their intuitions. (NYE JR. 2009:124-125)

Mourinho revealed his Contextual Intelligence when he arrived at Chelsea, compared with his arrival at FC Porto. If you remember, his appearance in FC Porto started with the promise. *"Next year, we'll be champions."* Mourinho made this promise for a simple reason. In Portugal, FC Porto's fans were accustomed to winning, it was the norm for the club to win and therefore it was an annual occurrence to compete for the national title. By promising the title, Mourinho respected the context of the last 20 years, despite the fact that the club had spent two and a half years without winning anything. That was a detail in the middle of the context.

When he arrived at Chelsea, the context was completely different. In its history, the London club had won just one league title and this had happened... 50 years earlier. Thus, the context was not one of victory, winning was not a habit and such a promise could be tricky, as well as creating pressure on his players.

Frank Lampard tells us how Mourinho handled the new context. After he arrived in England in 2004, Mourinho told the British journalists that the goal for that season would not be to win the Premier League, because that would be the season to adapt. However, that's not what he told his players:

"You will read in the press and hear in the media me saying that I don't expect us to win the league in my first season. I want you to be very clear that I have said this only to keep the pressure of all out of us." (Mourinho *in* Lampard 2006: 322)

With another approach, Deco's words also show an appreciation of Mourinho's Contextual Intelligence.

A coach must be a leader. Mourinho has it 100%, I have no doubts about that, so everything starts with leadership. However, I think a manager needs to have other qualities to be able to succeed, needs to master various aspects and Mourinho is good at all these aspects. To enumerate some of them I'll start with control over the press, knowing how to create a favourable environment for the players, knowing how to motivate them and at the same time relieve them from the outside pressure, managing the players' everyday issues, each with his character, his personality and his problems. In a group of 25 elements it's not easy, you have to be very attentive to detail... So I think Mourinho has this advantage, not only by coaching well tactically, in terms of preparation for matches etc., but also the cultural issue where he's inserted. Coaching in England is one thing, in Spain it's another, and in Italy it's another and so on... also, the remaining issues I've just mentioned and that have to do with what it takes to be a leader. If you add all this up, we can understand the success he has had throughout his life.

Another example also refers to the countries through which he passed as head coach. In all of them (England and Italy, excluding Portugal for obvious reasons) Mourinho introduced himself speaking the native language; it's a fact he could already speak English, but he had only a couple of months to learn Italian... and learned enough to understand the language and make himself clear.

6. TEAMS

One night, as we returned from a concert, we met our musician friend who asked us: 'Where do you come from?', to which we replied: 'We were in a concert of a famous orchestra.' He looked at us and asked another question. 'And did they play together or just at the same time?' (BINNEY ET AL, 2009: 41)

Everything I just described about José Mourinho's leadership cannot be read and interpreted out of context. I showed you that Mourinho's leadership exists only because there are followers willing to follow him, and to whom he has applied his leadership principles, as noted. By leading, José Mourinho has influenced, and by influencing, he has "led", according to his own terminology. Those followers he led turned into high performance teams.

So what is the value of the group/team[21] compared to the value of their individualities, since they only reach a high performance as a team? As I've clearly said before, the main idea for Mourinho is to make the group more valuable than the sum of its parts. To me, this is precisely the most intrinsic nature of groups (in Sport at least) whichever their purpose might be. Nowadays, nothing is achieved individually; only teams allow achievements that are beyond the reach of an individual by himself. The team has an added value compared to the sum of its parts. However, it's not enough to get together to form a team. Taking into account all the vast literature that triggers this issue, I opt for a simple definition that brings together the elements I consider essential for the framing of the issue.

---

[21] No distinction will be made between Group and Team. We shall treat this subject always with the same terminology, knowing that we are referring to high competition and high performance teams, precisely those that José Mourinho trains.

A team brings together people focused on a common goal working in a perfectly established way. It's defined as a group of organized individuals led by a leader and working within a context, towards the same objective. (DEVILLARD, 2001:33-34)

This definition involves the notions of a person in a team environment who needs a leader with a clear and definite goal, and who uses concerted practices of action.

Once we understand this notion, I don't hesitate to label the team a "living organism", as it acts and produces from interactions, relationships, connections, conversations and communication. This is how the team builds on itself and becomes a living organism. This is how it builds up a history and generates an idea for the future. What it becomes as a whole escapes the will of its individual members; what I want or aspire to may not be what the team wants and aspires to; the path can be different from what I want. This applies to me or to any of the other members as individuals. Thus, the team becomes a living organism changing and evolving over time, creating its own culture and personality regardless of individual desires. And so the team will always be something more, much more than the sum of its parts.

The parts may even just be "relatively" relevant when compared to the added value that the team adds to the simple value of the parts. So, we can understand what Mourinho means when he says that only the whole interests him. We can also understand what U2 drummer Larry Mullen told the television station SIC, when he was asked about the secret of the effectiveness and the success of U2:

The band members are partners, and we work as such. So we work together and share the song writing, everything at all levels... But I've always said that, although none of us had great musicianship (as seen, for example, with the big bands of R&B) we do have the capability to live / work in a band.

We're talking about one of the most successful bands active worldwide. We're talking about a 30-year-old band that has won more than 60 awards and sold about 145 million records in the whole world.

We're talking about success and longevity. Well, even Larry Mullen thinks that the members of U2 are not such high quality musicians. Like he said, the thing that makes them great, that sets them apart, that gives them success is *"their ability to work in a band"*. This means that the best don't make great teams, great teams make the best, those who achieve and maintain success. From another perspective, Mourinho also agrees with U2:

> *What strengthens a team is to play as a team. More important than having a great player or two great players is to play as a team. For me, this is very clear: the best team is not the one that has the best players, but one that plays as a team.*
>
> *To play as a team is to have organization, to have certain regularities that make all players have the same objective at the same time in the four moments of the game. But this is only possible with time, with work and with serenity. One thing is, the players realizing and trying to do what I want and the other is succeeding as a team. This takes time.* (OLIVEIRA ET AL, 2006: 191-92)

This is the kind of consciousness that seems very well founded in U2. Probably they have never studied teams or leadership, but their "praxis" leads them to assimilate what's important: *"the ability to work in a band"*. This is much more important than their individual "musicianship" which is not comparable to other great bands, according to Larry Mullen.

I can also include Didier Drogba's words about José Mourinho, in his autobiography:

> *Mourinho isn't a coach who trains players; he takes on people who are ready to adhere to his philosophy. What's more, they're not necessarily the best players in the world.* (DROGBA, 2008: 152)

So, it's easy to understand why the team is worth more than the sum of its parts and why the best elements may fail to generate the best teams; why the "galactic" Real Madrid never won anything and the "unknown" FC Porto won everything.

In light of Mourinho's leadership and the principles set out above, I will now address the issue of the high performance team created by José Mourinho. Basically, this answers the question: what kind of followers and team does José Mourinho's leadership model create?

THE FIRST "MOURINHO GROUP"

In the 2002/03 season, for the first time, José Mourinho built a team for a season from scratch and in his own way. In this case, FC Porto's team. He got some players from the previous season (not chosen by him, because he hadn't started the season, but that he felt gave him guarantees of a good job) and others he hired from some second line clubs (which don't fight for the title) as were the cases of Paulo Ferreira from Vitória de Setúbal, Pedro Emanuel from Boavista, Derlei, Tiago and Nuno Valente from União de Leiria.

It was a team built almost from scratch, with many new players who didn't know each other.

The early days of one of the most glorious campaigns ever were beginning for FC Porto and Mourinho told me, in his biography, in the chapter entitled "My Group":

The first week of work was very important, because the players who had gone to the World Cup [Japan and Korea] had not yet returned and these were largely those who had played in Porto the previous season, and that I already knew. I had a working week only with new players. I think that was very good for them. It allowed them to join the group and its working methods without the peer pressure of "heavy weight" players. This was important in terms of behaviour hesitation, which new guys always manifest. Without the 'old ones' they opened up more, were more genuine, which was highly positive, to getting to know them.

Moreover, regarding my methodology, I could start from scratch with them. It would've been more complicated with the others there. Imagine an exercise: for the 'old' players it would've been routine and for those who had just arrived it would be something new. It's like teaching English in a class where there are new students and others who have an advanced knowledge of the language. Here, the absence of some was beneficial to others. We could go to the essence of my exercises and even the vocabulary I sometimes use.

Then, when the others arrived, we went to train at Saint-Étienne in France. After three days of work I began to get feedback from the older players: 'Mister, there's a lot of quality in the new guys. Furthermore, the 'kids' are very good people...'"

And José Mourinho began to realize he was building a solid, cohesive group with future. The idea was reinforced after the fifth day of training.

That day, I gave them the afternoon and dinner time off. The only thing that I said was that I wanted them back at the hotel by 11pm. I didn't see them leave but I saw them coming in. I was with my assistants in the lobby waiting for them to return. It's usual to have people who come in late, because some players always prefer to pay a fine in order to arrive a little later. I was wrong. At about 20 minutes to 11 pm, I saw a taxi coming up with the first group of players inside. The other group arrived shortly after like a flash. I was astonished, not only because they arrived long before the appointed time, but also because they all came at the same time. I asked Jorge Costa, who was passing by me:

"Jorge, what has just happened here?"

"Mister, we were all together and we have a great group here."

(MOURINHO IN LOURENÇO 2004: 123)

This group was able to achieve feats as remarkable as unimaginable. Within two years, they won two national championships, a Portuguese Cup, the UEFA Cup and the Champions League.

THE TEAM AS A WHOLE

In Mourinho, the notion of team/group is viewed according to complexity, so the team is not just the sum of its component parts. It's more than that, but essentially it's not that (the sum of the parts).

The team (the whole) exists as an entity in itself and is not the sum or addition of other smaller entities (parts).

Let's imagine a group of 11 people to be a football team. At some point, a new manager arrives – the leader, if you will – bringing with him new ideas, new processes, new ways of working, and even new objectives. Although people are exactly the same, the team is now different because the connections, the relationships – professional and personal – among them have changed. The "whole" is different, in terms of interaction as well as identity. Looking only at the parts, the group remained unchanged; however, when we look at the "whole" we can see that it has changed substantially.

This concept fits with what was described when I referred to the human genome project. Just like humans, the group also differs, materializes and is comprised by the whole complex, rather than separate parts. Moreover, features may emerge from the group that are not found in any of the individual parts; however, they exist...

Hence, José Mourinho's answer when he was asked what his training philosophy is:

> Well, I'm a 'team coach' and I usually say, first of all, I don't teach my players how to play football, I teach them how to play as a team. Then, as a second purpose, I always want the whole to be more than the sum of its parts; therefore I am, I'll repeat, a 'team coach'. But I don't forget that I work with individuals, human beings. And each player is a different man, with their personality, way of being and living, with a different body, and because of that, I also need to look at them and work with them individually to get a maximum degree of efficiency from them for the benefit of the whole / team.

In the logic of inclusion that we have come to characterize José Mourinho's work, (where nothing is separate or out of context) we can see how his exercises during training are already designed and targeted to building and strengthening the team spirit – a kind of teambuilding. In other organizations, this is a task commissioned to other companies that are specialized in that work, and which is held on separate days out of the context of everyday work. In Mourinho, this comes naturally integrated in the day-to-day of his team. Let's see 3 examples:

Exercise 1   Mourinho puts 10 players playing against another 10 (the number is irrelevant). When he whistles, one element of a team comes out and must work around an object that is at a considerable distance. Soon after, another whistle, and another player of the same team leaves. This situation makes the team lose two players momentarily. If the players go around the obstacle faster, they will have less time. This exercise, apart from requiring time management of the ones who stay (it's different if they are in possession of the ball or without it, winning or losing, etc.) forces those who leave to make an additional effort for the team and its sacrifice because, the faster they are, the sooner they return to the team, and they lessen the sacrifice of their teammates who are playing with two fewer players than the opposition.

Exercise 2   Also in the game, the rule is simple: a player who has the ball can only touch it once, the following player can touch it as many times as he likes and so on. What does this exercise accomplish? The player who has the ball always tries to worry about his teammate rather than himself. If he just touches the ball once, he always postpones the difficult part, which is precisely touching the ball once. If I pass the ball after the first touch, my teammate can give as many touches as he likes, until he passes the ball. He won't find himself in the limit of only being able to touch a ball once, because I already gave several.

Exercise 3   In another game, left-footed players can only play with their right foot and right-footed players can only play with their left foot. This demands that my main concern is always passing the ball to my teammates in an ideal situation for their weakest leg. While playing, I have to think about my teammate and the way I'll pass the ball and not about myself.

We can take two basic teachings that once learned, lead to leadership effectiveness: people are complex and people are different.

This introduction, quite informative in my opinion, serves to situate the analysis of Mourinho's group as he sees it, and as he builds it, necessarily different from the analysis of others who look for the group through a reductionist angle. Thus, we can also understand Mourinho's perspective of his group: it is, as he himself says, more important than any part, and so he sacrifices any part for the group. Therefore, the group is the "star" rather than any player; in other words, all players are equal before the group and the group, which is much more and much different than the sum of parts, is the real star, the one capable of reaching the objectives, or not. Therefore, referring to the example that opens this chapter, the choice of the elements of the group must be fully comprehensive regardless the professional qualities of the elements in question:

> *Now, in Porto's caravan, good players are not the only ones who get in. With José Mourinho, it was opted to also perform a careful analysis of the men's moral qualities. Besides good players, we also looked for good men, because quality must emerge from the group as a whole, given that football is a collective sport. In order to work, a team must be composed by men of character, who look for the group as something more important than each isolated individual. Only the group matters and only the group is important to maintain.* (LOURENÇO 2004: 123-124)

It was in this way, with these principles, that Mourinho explained to me how he sees the group's value before the value of the individual:

> *To me the whole is everything, the part is an important means for the whole to achieve its objectives. So I think that from the time that group culture exists, there's the culture of the whole. The overall objective is perfectly acculturated by the group. I think the notion of 'sacrificing the part for the whole' stops making any sense. It's through the parts that you reach the whole. So for me, in all aspects of training and complexity of my mission as the leader of a group, the whole is the only thing that interests me.*

In the parts within his group, Mourinho is looking for global consistency with this overall premise of: values, methods, principles and thinking. This consistency is well mirrored in his philosophy when, for the first time in his career, in the 2002/03 season, he built FC Porto's team from scratch: Mourinho was looking for players who were ambitious, poor and without any trophies (Lourenço 2003). FC Porto was built around this central idea and, for the two years that followed, they would win all the titles they took part in – with the exception of a Portuguese Cup and a UEFA Super Cup. For this purpose, it's irrelevant what kind of player Mourinho wanted. What we want to highlight is that Mourinho wanted to create a group of equals among equals, where there weren't any economic, personal, technical, or any other discrepancies. For Mourinho, only this overall uniformity could build the group, only in the group could each of the players see their technical, physical, economic, etc. capabilities, improved; only this uniformity could give a future to the group.

Being so crosscutting, this group concept applies to completely different groups with the same effectiveness.

Let's go back to the group U2, which in 2009 celebrated their 30-year career anniversary. Before they gave a concert in Portugal that same year, the Irish group gave an interview to the television channel SIC. When asked about the secret of the band's longevity, front man Bono said: *"The temptation that we have managed to avoid so far, the one I'm most proud of was the creation and development of 'individual egos' that are always the source of band breakups."*

We also detect the concern for this uniformity and homogeneity in Bono's words. In other words, it's the only way to avoid the emergence of the so-called "individual egos" or "stardom". Therefore, U2 have celebrated 30 years of success, a somewhat unique union in the music world. Almost three years after Mourinho's departure, Chelsea manages to stay on top of worldwide competitiveness, even if it remains virtually the same team – except for two or three players – that Mourinho built. This circumstance becomes more exceptional because Chelsea have had four managers after Mourinho.

Again, we emphasize the essence of the matter: reality is not defined by divided and separated parts but rather by their connections and relations. It's easy to understand Mourinho's main purpose when he builds and maintains a group: homogeneity among the parts, always in a relational field and in the context of the whole.

Based on this inter and intra relational logic, José Mourinho explained to me how he builds and develops a team, namely, a high competition team, or high performance, if you will:

When building a team, I must try to hide the bad qualities of this team, I must try to hide the bad qualities of the players and I always need to have this idea present. However good the team is, however good the players are, regardless of the level of performance the team has achieved, all teams, all players, all systems, all models have flaws and qualities. As far as the players, I'm trying to take advantage of their qualities and hide their shortcomings. I want them to know not only what their strengths and weaknesses are, but also know the strengths and weaknesses of their teammates.

On the other hand, in a tactical structure of 11 there is a physical proximity in relation to each other. The centre-back has a right-back on his right, another centre-back on his left, one or two defensive midfielders in front of him and the goalkeeper behind him. As a centre-back I have to know, for example, that my winger usually loses balls under pressure, so I can't play with him when the opponent is pressing the team. I know that the centre-back playing beside me is a slow player and as such I have to pay attention to balls played in behind him to give him proper cover. I have to know that my goalkeeper doesn't know how to kick with his left foot, so I can't give him the ball on the foot he can't play with. However, I also have to learn that my goalkeeper is fantastic with high balls, so we should try to force our opponent to cross high because this is a comfortable situation for us, due to the efficacy of our goalkeeper. Anyway, players must have all this information so they can play according to the characteristics of each of their teammates.

When I was at Chelsea, I always said to my central defenders: if Makelele is playing in front of you, go into the midfield with the ball because, if you lose it, Makelele will be where he has to be to cover the void you left when you left the defence; if Essien is in the midfield don't go in there with the ball, because Essien will chase you and if you lose the ball, there will be no one there when the opponent has the ball. The players have to understand the functional connections that exist in the game according to the characteristics of others around them. To conclude, I think it's fundamental we all know those around us, and in a concerted, relational and systemic manner, everybody has to contribute to the whole, the organization, whichever type it is.

And just when the topic is the creation and development of a team and the relationship among its elements, the quote of Marcia Hughes and James Terrell, in their book *The Emotionally Intelligent Team*, may help us to better understand and classify Mourinho's words.

The more they know each other, the easier it is to trust and the more reasons exist for them to do so. The real value of building team relationships is when everyone understands more about how each one became what they are, different customs, sensitive points, strengths, challenges and passions create synergy and understanding, leading to better outcomes and better practices. It allows them to help each other to compensate and respond with greater flexibility and resilience, transforming the stress of change (...) regarding the situation, [the team members] stand together. It is the birthplace of an extraordinary team.

(HUGHES, TERREL, 2009: 202-3)

Drogba's words, although framed differently, also help us understand this problem.

He knows how to lead the team, how to lead a group of people, how to make people come together, how to involve them... how to motivate them. I think he understands something very important: in order to have good results you have to be psychologically fit. So he understands that you have to give something to the players for them to be in perfect psychological conditions. If this is accomplished, players will surely reciprocate. And Mourinho is almost perfect on this subject.

Tactically, he is the best, on the pitch, he's also very good during the match, but with regard to mental preparation of players he's very intelligent, brilliant.

It is from these kinds of notions that Mourinho intuitively introduces his group culture. To Edgar H. Shein (2004), the guru of "organizational culture", the culture of an organization or a group, is made up by its values, its ideology, the reason why people are there, the way they are and how they are. In Mourinho, the first trace of this culture, which is also understood outside his group, is precisely the supremacy of the group over the individual. Consider Shevchenko's words to an Italian newspaper, before he started working at Chelsea: *"On this team, I'm available for whatever [Mourinho] wants."* We consider superstar Shevchenko's tacit acceptance of the ideology of Mourinho's group, i.e. his willingness to do the work that the coach wants in favour of the group and collective success. This is the goal, the success of the group rather than the individual's, the *"reason of being of those who are there, the way they are and how they are"*. It's a culture based on the success of the group and not on the success around the "star", as for example, at Real Madrid, where the players were and are dubbed "galacticos". In Mourinho, the group is the galactic one and the parts know it very well.

In the conversation I had with Jorge Costa, he justified "Mourinho's culture" precisely through success materialized in a culture of victory:

> *I think a lot depends on the cultures of each country where he is a manager, but I think that, after some time, there is always a 'Mourinho culture', especially when we speak of a culture of victory.*

With this culture, Mourinho helps to foster and maintain a factor he considers crucial to the performance of the group: unity or cohesion of the group. As a complex whole, his group is a cohesive, united and supportive whole. Even outside the football pitch, the group must remain a group, based on their values, which don't disappear or take a break when not performing their work.

Solidification, performance, maintaining the values are built in all acts of life of each of the parts, with no differences between professional and social life. So we could see on TV, the entire Chelsea squad go to the hospital to visit their goalkeeper, Petr Cech, after he had suffered a serious head injury during a Premiership match, which raised the question of his professional future. This also explains how Mourinho advocates solidarity among the members of his group at the service of its cohesion and unity. If Mourinho wants supportive players, he can't adopt a tactical man-to-man marking, which doesn't promote mutual aid and solidarity at all.

Regarding the rules Mourinho implemented as soon as he arrived at Chelsea, Barclay wrote (2005:183): *"He insisted that the players had to behave as a unit on and off the pitch."* However, besides the group as a whole, Mourinho also promotes another decisive factor for success in his groups. This is what he usually refers to as *winning mentality*, which we can call a "culture of winning". For this analysis, it's clear that, in terms of cultural consistency of Mourinho's groups, it's the victory in each and every match that can balance them. The whole and each of its parts, i.e., the Chelsea team as a group, and its individual players are balanced by their victories.

Let us recall some previously quoted examples. One of them is evident when he spoke to FC Porto's players following the defeat at home to Panathinaikos. By sending them the message that those who didn't believe in the victory wouldn't play again in Greece, Mourinho sought to balance the parts that, in psychological terms, were reacting to the defeat badly rather than balancing the whole (Lourenço 2003). The players got the message: you only win by believing you can win. The players believed it, and after the balance among the parts came the balance of the whole crowned with their victory in Greece.

Another example relates to Frank Lampard. This is part of a dialogue between coach and player, described in the book *Totally Frank*, the English player's biography: *"You are just as good as Zidane, Vieira or Deco and now all you have to do is win things. You are the best player in the world but now you need to prove it and win trophies."* (Lampard 2006: 311) When Mourinho told him he was the best player in the world, but he would have to win trophies to have recognition, he clearly showed him that one thing couldn't be separated from the other. Lampard had an imbalance that had to do with quality versus effectiveness, and balance can only be achieved when quality and effectiveness go together. In order for Lampard to go down in history, a theoretical recognition of his value was not enough; he would have to get the practical recognition embodied in victory.

This culture of victory, of "only victory matters" or "the second is the first of the last" is another recognized factor in Mourinho, which explains the high motivational level that exists in all his groups.

However, a group isn't formed spontaneously. There are several steps to go through, since its formation up to the stage of full maturity, and it is up to the leader to keep a watchful eye on that development.

Now, it interests us to know how Mourinho develops and maintains his group at its most mature stage, precisely in view of the continuous equilibrium. The question is: will Mourinho be different here, as well? The answer isn't easy, because our analysis is not comparative. However, Mourinho's leadership in this field gives us some ideas, especially in the first phase of the group development (membership) and the last (collaboration). We focus on these two for two reasons: as we shall see in the next paragraph, we consider them of paramount importance because, in both cases, either their assumptions materialize or the group will not exist. The initial phase (membership) presupposes the creation of the group; if it doesn't happen, the group won't exist. If the final phase (collaboration) doesn't consolidate the group, it will crumble. The intermediate stages are essentially aimed at the relationships, at the connections among the elements of the group, which may be better or worse but, generally, the continuity of the group does not depend on them to maintain itself.

Mourinho pays notorious attention to the initial phase of the group. As I said before, when he chose and developed his first group (FC Porto's team in 2002/03 season), Mourinho started training as soon as the players got together for the first time: *After three days of work I began to get feedback from the oldest [players]: 'Boss, there's a lot of quality in the new guys.'"* (Mourinho *in* Lourenço 2004: 123) It was no accident that Mourinho insisted in recording this passage in his biography. It reflects the manager's concern about the integration of the new members of his group, as well as his concern at this stage of its formation. That's why Mourinho describes in detail the first day off of FC Porto's training. The players left training together, dined together and came back to the hotel together on their own volition. Upon their arrival, Mourinho was waiting for them and heard team captain Jorge Costa tell him: *"We were all together and we have a great group here."* (Lourenço 2004: 123) Mourinho commented this event:

> *It's hard to express the feelings of a coach when he hears the captain saying these things. Twenty or so men who had been together for just five days, chose to remain together, eat and socialize on their first day off. My group was arising.* (MOURINHO IN LOURENÇO 2004: 123)

Let us now consider the situation with the theory of group development proposed by Obert (1979), one of the authors I studied and whose theory may be applied to this topic. According to the author, this first phase (membership) is characterized by early contacts, when people tend to be more concerned about themselves than about the group, and the environment can become tense. At this stage, according to Obert, the leader's role is crucial because his task is facilitating and promoting knowledge among people. Mourinho's role is clear: his group was beginning there, and it didn't remain united and cohesive only in the first five days of work. It remained this way in the first break of its elements, outside of work.

Another thing about Mourinho's selection for the creation of his group: let's say that this is a pre-group creation phase, so there is no question about its development yet, but we consider it essential for its subsequent creation. What are Mourinho's criteria for the selection of the elements of his group? We can find the answer in his biography, which I have already mentioned above, although in a different context. We continue with FC Porto's team, during the 2002/03 season:

> *With José Mourinho, we also opted to carry out a thorough analysis of the men's moral qualities. Besides good players, we sought good men, because the quality must emerge from the group as a whole, as football is a collective sport.* (LOURENÇO 2004: 123-4)

Mourinho's attention to issues pertaining to the group, as we've said, is not reduced to its initial phase. Let's go to the final phase proposed by Obert (1979), the collaboration that, according to the investigator, very few groups can reach. This is the full maturity stage of a group, when all other stages have been fully overcome. The group is experiencing a stable period. However, this stability can cause problems. So let's see an example that happened with José Mourinho which gives us a full view of his special attention to the moments, even when his entire group is working very effectively.

The 2002/03 season ended with FC Porto victorious on all fronts: in the Portuguese Championship, in the Portuguese Cup and in the UEFA Cup. The following season, Mourinho maintained the structure of this group with only minor changes. The "machine" was tuned, everyone knew each other, and everyone could play with their eyes closed. But at the start of the new season, Mourinho was assaulted by a question: did success hurt us? (Lourenço 2004). Far from living the victories of the recent past, Mourinho was already focused on future victories and didn't get carried away by the environment of euphoria. Fearing a negative reaction to success on the part of his players, the manager took action at the tactical level by "forcing" his players to "come down to earth" and focusing only on what was to come, rather than what had happened. This way, we can understand how Mourinho maintained a winning team and the result was in sight: at the end of the season, Mourinho and his team won the Portuguese League and the Champions League. So, we can also understand how Mourinho manages a coherent, consistent and visible course, a "common logic" if you will, with every one of his teams. Hence, Didier Drogba's words, which I transcribe, when I asked him whether there really was a "Mourinho culture" in his teams. Didier replied with an instructive example.

Yes, I think there is. Would you like me to give you an example? Two weeks ago, I played against Inter Milan (managed by Mourinho) and it was interesting because I saw Inter and was watching the Chelsea of his time, it was unbelievable. That way of playing, of being on the pitch, of playing the game, the intensity put in the game. They suffered a goal and immediately searched for the equalizer and got it just a few minutes later. The intelligence with which they competed in the match, the organization they demonstrated, their objectiveness... admittedly, they didn't play well, but that was Mourinho's Chelsea.

Mourinho's Porto, Mourinho's Chelsea, Mourinho's Inter... Inevitably, sooner or later, the teams that José Mourinho trains are known and recognized by journalists, football professionals, Sports' scholars and anonymous citizens who just love football. These are Mourinho's teams, not in the sense of belonging, but the way they play, above all, an identifiable personality, a culture and a leadership that make José Mourinho a unique manager.

EPILOGUE

This book was based on my Masters Degree's thesis, which was about Mourinho's leadership. I've developed some new ideas, and abandoned others that didn't convince me anymore. I had the help of several friends and transcribed new and unpublished interviews by José Mourinho, Vítor Baía, Jorge Costa, Deco and Didier Drogba. I tried to make the overall work of Mourinho easy to read and to understand, with special focus – the *dominant*, according to his own terminology – on his leadership. However, no one reading this book will be a second Mourinho in the "art" of leadership. Surely not. There's no use trying to copy it because, under the principles of complexity, you can't.

I merely presented a leadership model in a pragmatic way, as far as possible. A leadership model that I consider new and think José Mourinho is a pioneer of. For the first time, at least in top-level competitive sport, someone materialised the complexity theory in a quite satisfactory degree. And this, as we've demonstrated, is a winning model that produced fantastic results in a very short space of time, and it's precisely this model that any of us can follow. However, in doing so, you'll use your personal style, your unique mark, because each of us is unique. It is this oneness that we have to follow when we talk about leadership. This is his plea and his history: no two leaders are alike.

Nowadays, we all face the challenge of leadership, because we are either leaders or followers. The complex competitive environment of the 21st century demands courageous, bold leaders who are "one step ahead", not cautious administrators who only know day-to-day management. Leadership today is about taking responsibility and risks, pointing out ways and being ready for self-sacrifice for one's followers. Only this can inspire others and get their best efforts.

For me, José Mourinho is one of those examples of effective leadership. The results obtained by the teams led or guided by him speak for themselves. I'm well aware that results are not everything, but there can be no good leaders without good results. Mourinho has won consistently and stubbornly and will continue to win, precisely because he is consistent. His ambition is unlimited and renews itself with every victory, it rebuilds itself at every step, and he instils effects in his followers. We have seen how men who have not worked with Mourinho for many years still talk about him, and the essentially relevant "way" they speak of him. The fascination Mourinho caused them, everything he taught them and the trophies they won with him, marked Baía, Jorge Costa, Deco and Drogba deeply. We can see that Mourinho's leadership is still present in their lives, in their way of being and seeing the world .

Someone asked me in one of my classes: "When you studied Mourinho did you hear anything that contradicted you?"

This question was important to dispel doubts about the type of work I did. First of all, we must retain the precise notion that this is not a journalistic work. We're not even dealing with a scientific work, as was the case of my Masters Degree's thesis. This work is no longer a thesis, although it started as one. I follow all the laws of ethics, of serious and applied study but this doesn't have – nor did I want it to – scientific proof, as it is generally understood. I discovered and developed some new ideas but always in a completely free way, following my conscience. Nor – and for the first time – did I let Mourinho read what I wrote. Even now, as I write these words, José Mourinho has not read a single line yet.

I listened to whom I thought was important. From what they told me, I selected what I thought was most striking to help us understand Mourinho's leadership. I started with preconceived ideas about leadership that I had already studied and, therefore, I got engaged in a "guided discovery": I knew where I was going but I didn't have the exact notion of what would lie ahead until I got there. This book is the product of this road, of this new fascinating journey through the rails of Mourinho's leadership – the last on this subject about Mourinho – and different from what I imagined at first. Neither better nor worse, just different. And I like it that way.

If anyone takes some advantage of any kind whatsoever from it, I'll feel accomplished, I'll feel that it was worth it. To all of those who have read it, my gratitude.

LUÍS LOURENÇO
MARCH 24, 2010